Mysteries of Joy

PHILIP KRILL

ISBN: 978-1-4834-7528-8 (sc)
ISBN: 978-1-4834-7527-1 (e)

Lulu Publishing Services rev. date: 10/20/2017

To

Mary Howell

She who comes in peace, always bringing joy!

CONTENTS

INTRODUCTION

The Rosary is the prayer of the gospel. It is the gospel first heard and experienced by Mary, the Mother of God, Proto-type of the Church. "Blessed is she who believed that there would be a fulfillment of what was spoken to her by the Lord' (Lk. 1:45). Mary believed before anyone else. She believed more perfectly than anyone else. It is for this reason that she is memorialized by Scripture: "Henceforth, all generations will call me blessed" (Lk. 1:48).

We are commanded by the Word of God to call Mary "blessed." This should give our fundamentalist brethren pause. Mary is insepa-rable from Jesus, just as the Word is inseparable from the Response. The Father gave Jesus His humanity in and through Mary. The instrument of our salvation – the sacred humanity of Jesus - comes from the womb of His mother. His blood is her blood. She is, to quote St. Irenaeus, "the cause of our salvation."[1] Her perfect re-sponse to the angel Gabriel's invitation to become the Mother of God makes the Blessed Virgin Mary both the model and inspiration of those who know themselves to be saved by grace working through faith (Eph. 2:8; cf. Rom. 5:1; Gal. 2:16).

As the perfect model of faith, Mary is also the fulfillment of the faith of Abraham (Gen. 15:6; cf. Rom. 4:22). Our blessed "father in faith," Abraham (Rom. 4:16), finds his completion in our Blessed Mother, Mary. It is important to remember in this connection that all humanity is "feminine" vis-à-vis God. Mary is the first and foremost

---

[1] *Against Heresies*, III, 22, 4.

to believe in Jesus as the Son of God. In faith, she offers her Son to His Father in sacrifice (Lk. 2:22; cf. Gen. 22:1-19). She is called upon to complete in action what Abraham was asked to do only in intention. She perfects on Calvary what Abraham was "reckoned as righteous" for being willing to do at Moriah. Hence, her faith is the fulfillment and completion of his.

Jesus is unthinkable without the person of Mary. Just as Adam is inseparable from Eve in the tragedy of sin, Jesus is inseparable from Mary in the drama of salvation. God's offer of redemption in Christ is impossible without the human response of Mary in the name of fallen humanity. Without this personal, human response, the gospel is null and void. Mary said Yes! for all of creation. The fruitfulness of the Word-made-flesh for the entire cosmos (cf. Jn. 6:33) came about because of Mary's quiet assent in the tiny village of Nazareth. "Blessed is she who believed that there would be a fulfillment of what was spoken to her by the Lord' (Lk. 1:45).

Through the ages, metaphors abound for Mary's symbiotic relationship with the Redeemer. Jesus is the sun, Mary is the moon. Jesus is the wine, Mary the chalice.[2] The point of all these images is that some of the most profound dimensions of the Mystery of Jesus can be known in no other way than through contemplation of Mary. Gazing into her face, we see His. Seeing Him through her eyes, we learn to see Him more perfectly. He is all the better known the more closely we draw near to the one who bore Him.

The inseparability of Mary from Jesus is a mystery as important as it is difficult to grasp. Jesus' intimacy with and dependence upon His mother is the human equivalent of His union with His Father and their Holy Spirit. Jesus' divine and human natures are hypostatically inseparable in His Incarnation. But these "natures" are more personally rooted and reflected in his relationship with Mary.

In the early third century, St. Cyprian said, "He is not able to

---

[2] cf. Hymn, *Mary The Dawn Christ The Perfect Day*.

have God as his Father who doesn't have the Church as mother."[3] The same is true for the Christian vis-à-vis Mary: One is not able to have Jesus as their Lord and Savior who doesn't have Mary as his or her mother as well. Know Mary, know Jesus. No Mary, no real comprehension of Jesus.

Relationality is of the essence of God. As Christians we do not believe in a monolithic deity. Generic theism is not for us. We are Trinitarian to the core. God is for us always and only: Father, Son, and Holy Spirit. Relationship is not an add-on or afterthought in the Life of the Trinity. Father, Son, and Holy Spirit were not first individual Persons who subsequently decided to form communion. No, they are inseparable from all eternity. They never were without each other. Their entire and individual identities are defined by their relationships with each other. These relationships constitute their separateness as divine Persons within the Trinitarian *Koinonia*. They are distinct Persons bound together in an eternally inseparable and indissoluble union. Wherever they go, whatever they do, they go and do together. And to whomever they come, they invite into their Trinitarian *Perichoresis*.[4]

For the Eternal Word to become flesh, the Father sent the Holy Spirit who overshadowed the Blessed Virgin Mary (Lk. 1:35). She was "chosen and predestined before the foundation of the world to be holy and blameless in His sight" (cf. Eph. 1:4; Lk. 1:75). She was specially formed, selected, and invited to become the 2nd Eve, the Mother of all the living. She was elected by the Father to be the New Ark of the New Covenant. She was perfected in every way by the Father's prevenient grace. She is, in the words of the poet, "our tainted race's solitary boast."[5]

Through the power of the Holy Spirit, the Word united Himself

---

[3] St. Cyprian, *On the Unity of the Catholic Church*, 6.

[4] περιχώρησις: describes the relationship between each person of the triune God (Father, Son, and Holy Spirit) as a co-inherent, eternally dynamic 'circulation' of love. The word *circumincession* is also used to convey the same idea.

[5] William Wordsworth, *The Virgin*.

to His mother with the same inseparable love with which He enjoys eternally with His Father. Jesus is inseparable from those He loves, whether in heaven above or on earth. "Inseparability" and "communion" are synonyms for the divine nature. We are "partakers of the divine nature" (2 Pt. 1:4) through the Father's predilection. Mary is the first and foremost instance of the human race saying Yes to the Father's final and definitive offer of salvation. Her Fiat (Lk. 1:38) is the key that opens the door to our restoration to our Original Unity with Him.[6] As the 2nd Eve, Mary's obedience and faith untangles the knots of disobedience and disbelief with which our first parents bound the human race in sin. The typological comparisons of Mary to Eve, recounted from Irenaeus to Newman, are no pious parallels, no empty allegories.[7] They contain an Incarnational and Trinitarian truth upon which all orthodox Christian faith and practice is established. If Mary is not the Mother of God, Jesus is not divine. If Jesus is not divine, we have not been saved.

But Mary is more, even, than the Mother of God (*Theotokos*). She has a unique relationship with each of the Persons of the Trinity. She is the *Daughter* of the Father, *Mother* of the Son, and *Spouse* of the Holy Spirit. By entering into the mystery of Mary's differing relationships with each of the Persons of the Trinity, we are able to understand certain things about God's relationship with us and within Himself that we can appreciate in no other way.

Recall that Adam and Eve were created freely and gratuitously by God for communion with Him who is Communion within Himself: Father, Son, and Holy Spirit. Our creation as man and woman – the specific form of His image and likeness (Gen. 1:26) – is for the sole and express purpose of sharing in the ecstatic love that circulates among Father, Son, and Holy Spirit. The one-flesh union enjoyed by our first parents in the Garden was the natural overflow and

---

[6] See John Paul II, *Man and woman He created them: A Theology of the Body*. 156-167.

[7] St. Irenaeus, *Against the Heresies*, 3.22.4; John Henry Newman, *An Essay on the Development of Christian Doctrine*, 196-296.

expression – the surplus and the symbol – of their participation in Divine love. The ecstasy of their nuptial union was, for Adam and Eve – as it is meant to be for Christian married couples living in God's Embrace in the sacrament of marriage – as a sacred connection, not only between themselves, but also, and most importantly, with the triune God. Marital love – indeed, all human love and friendship – exists purely and simply as a trinitarian gift intended to reflect and connect those of us who enjoy it with the Trinitarian God who created us in His love and for His love. All such love and connection – both human and divine – was lost through the disobedience and infidelity of Adam and Eve. All such love and happy communion is now restored though the obedience and fidelity of Jesus and Mary.

I am very well aware, as I write these lines in praise of Mary, that it seems altogether too much for the non-Catholic frame of mind. Still more irksome to my Protestant friends is the medieval maxim, "No praise of Mary is ever enough."[8] How are we to reconcile these colliding views of Mary? How are we to appeal to non-Catholic Christians who believe, in their dialectical way of imagining the relation of God and the world,[9] that we make too much of Mary, even to the point of idolatry?

Books of Catholic apologetics abound, making the 'case for Mary[10] But from the perspective of this book, a Marian apologetic is counter-productive. The best apologetics, in our opinion, is the apologetics of beauty and the apologetics of holiness. In other words, it is the apologetics of Mary herself. We need only contemplate the mysteries in the life of Mary with Jesus and the truth of Mary for our appreciation and union with the Blessed Trinity will become

---

[8] For a balanced and scholarly approach to Marian devotion see Joseph Ratzinger, *Daughter Zion: Meditations on the Church's Marian Belief*, 72-82.

[9] For a revealing contrast between the Catholic 'analogical imagination' and the Protestant 'dialectical mindset,' see Mark S. Massa S.J., *Anti-Catholicism in America: The Last Acceptable Prejudice*.

[10] See, e.g., Father Mateo, *Refuting the Attack on Mary*.

apparent. It is never enough to quote the countless Church Fathers, saints, and Catholic converts in praise of Mary to convince the person's whose mind is closed to Jesus' mother, of her indispensability to Him. Ultimately, Mary needs no defense. "She alone," says St. Bernard of Clairvaux, "has defeated all heresies."[11]

In what follows we will look at Mary as through a prism towards the Trinity. She is never pointing to herself. She is always revealing her Son. Her only command is "Do whatever He tells you" (Jn. 2:5). In directing us to Jesus, she is also commending us to the Father and the Holy Spirit. She is Our Lady of the Trinity. Looking at her and listening to what the Spirit reveals to us about the mysteries of her life with Jesus, we may be surprised to find how deeply the Father draws us into His own Trinitarian Life.

A Note on Method

The following 50 meditations represent a Scriptural Rosary done in *lectio divina* style. Each Hail Mary for all 5 decades of the Mysteries of Joy will be preceded by a contemplative meditation on a single line from Scripture related to the Mystery at hand. The Scripture passages used are those typically associated with the Scriptural Rosary. May it please God that the following reflections render adequate praise to Mary, the Mystical Rose, and glorify the Father, Son, and Holy Spirit who have chosen her specially to communicate their salvation to our fallen world.

---

[11] For a modern interpretation of this medieval maxim, see Joseph Ratzinger and Hans Urs von Balthasar, *Mary: The Church at the Source*, 25-26.

Annunciation

"The angel Gabriel was sent from God to a city of Galilee named Nazareth, to a virgin betrothed to a man named Joseph, of the house of David; and the virgin's name was Mary."

This is the first we hear of Mary. We see she is the object of several persons' attention. God, first of all, initiates action with Mary for reasons known only to Him. We must presume these reasons to be pre-eminently important. He is making a special election of Mary. It is an election directly related to His Son; therefore, it is an action, and an election, that is greater than the sum of all previous acts of election on His part, including the call of Abraham and the choice of Israel as His inviolately sacred people.

Then there is Gabriel. He is commanded by God to deliver His revelation and His request to the virgin of Nazareth. Gabriel is perfectly suited for this task. He has proven himself God's loyal messenger eons before in eternity when he resisted the rebellion of Satan and other heavenly minions and, together with the other good angels, demonstrated his unyielding devotion to the Most High God. He is exceptionally equipped to deliver the Father's invitation to Mary to cooperate in His final and most important act on behalf of humanity by becoming the Mother of His only-begotten Son.

Joseph is the next person who appears. We know little about Joseph, save apocryphal speculation that he was a widower with children before being betrothed to Mary.[12] But Joseph is by no means

---

[12] The chief sources of information on the life of St. Joseph are the first chapters of our first and third Gospels; they are practically also the only reliable sources. In most instances it is next to impossible to discern and sift these particles of true history

unimportant. He is a key figure in the tableau God is constellating for the advent of His Son. Joseph is the secure context for all that will transpire if Mary is disposed to accept God's dramatic proposal. He is Mary's human spouse, but the Holy Spirit will be her divine Spouse. Similarly, Joseph will be Jesus' human father, but Yahweh will show Himself to be Our Lord's heavenly Father (Lk. 3:22; cf. Mt. 3:17; 17:5; Mk. 1:11; 9:7).

Last of all we encounter Mary. She seems diminutive by contrast to what has been happening around her. We see clearly how everything has been "arranged" for her, all has been done "to" her. She is the object of arrangements made for her without her consent. She is on the receiving end of actions that were beyond her control: she is chosen by God, accosted by Gabriel, betrothed to Joseph, and embedded in the house of David. Nothing remains, it seems, for her except her consent.

But it is precisely here that we first glimpse the mystery and beauty of Mary. She is a virgin...she has a name..."and the virgin's name was Mary." What's in a name? Mary means "beloved." Mary is "God's beloved." We know from Scripture (cf. Gen. 32:27) that a person's name reveals his or her unique qualities and role in the eyes of God. God grants persons a change of name when His mission for them is made know through revelation (cf. Gen. 17:5, 15; 32:28; Acts 13:9).[13] Mary's name needed no change. She is always and forever "God's beloved." And for reasons that will become clear as we move further into our contemplation of Mary's uniqueness, Mary defines the meaning of "beloved," the adjective does not define the person of Mary. Mary is "God's beloved" because of *who* He created her to be. She is no mere instance of other "beloveds of God" whose names

---

from the fancies with which they are associated. Among the apocryphal productions dealing more or less extensively with some episodes of St. Joseph's life are the so-called "*Gospel of James*", the "*Pseudo-Matthew*", the "*Gospel of the Nativity of the Virgin Mary*", the "*Story of Joseph the Carpenter*", and the "*Life of the Virgin and Death of Joseph*".
[13] On the relation of name to identity and mission, see Joseph Cardinal Ratzinger, *Principles of Catholic Theology: Building Stones for a Fundamental Theology*, 68-69.

may or may not be 'Mary'. The virgin of Nazareth named "Mary" – the one and only person "betrothed to Joseph" – she, and no one else, is chosen by God for what He intends to accomplish for the world through the Incarnation of His Eternal Word. The Mary we encounter in this first mention of her in Scripture is *unsubstitutable* for who and what God intends her to be and do. Far from being unimportant, Mary is indispensable to the Father's plan of salvation. She is as indefinable and irreplaceable to the Father's redemptive mystery as is the Son Whom He will send to be hers as well.

It is an egregious desecration of the Christological mystery to think of Mary as an indifferent instrument or mechanical piece in the providence of God. Far worse is the fundamentalist élan to regard the Blessed Mother as an impersonal womb or convenient birth canal for the arrival of the Savior. If any womb other than hers would have sufficed to give birth to Jesus, the crowds that followed Him would not have exclaimed, "Blessed is the womb that bore you, and the breasts at which you nursed" (Lk. 11:27). And if any person other than Mary would have sufficed to assent to her mission, Jesus would not have responded in praise of His mother when He exclaimed, "Blessed are they [in imitation of Mary] who hear the Word of God and abide by it" (Lk. 8:21).[14] As St. Augustine

---

[14] "He was told, 'Your mother and your brothers are standing outside and they wish to see you.' He said to them in reply, 'My mother and my brothers are those who hear the word of God and act on it'" (Lk. 8:20–21). This is a Scripture passage often misinterpreted as a criticism of Mary. As Joseph Ratzinger says, "These statements are only apparently anti-Marian. In reality, the texts proffer two extremely important insights. First, over and above Christ's once-only physical birth, there is another dimension of motherhood that can and must continue further. Second, this motherhood, which brings Christ to birth again and again, rests upon the hearing, keeping, and doing of Jesus' word. Now, it is the same Luke from whose Gospel the two above-mentioned sayings are cited who portrays Mary as the archetypal hearer of the Word, who bears the Word, keeps it, and brings it to maturity. This means that, in handing on these sayings of the Lord, Luke is not denying veneration of Mary; he is, rather, attempting to set it on its true foundation. He shows that Mary's maternity is not simply a uniquely occurring biological event; he shows, rather, that she was and, therefore, also remains a mother with her whole person. This becomes

reminds us, "Mary conceived Jesus in her heart before she conceived Him in her womb."[15]

Thus we see, in this very first verse introducing us to Mary, the indispensability of this woman to the conquest of sin by Christ in the eternal plan of the Father (cf. Gen. 3:15). In one sense everything was predetermined: she is wedded to Joseph, God the Father has chosen her, the angel Gabriel has addressed her...yet, everything "holds its breath" until Mary begins to speak.[16] Mary has been the object of divine, angelic, and human activity, but it is as a subject with free will, deep emotion, and singular personality that Mary matters unconditionally in the mystery of our salvation. Nothing can move forward until we know how it stands with Mary. All is prepared, but nothing can be consummated until Mary consents. In a manner that confounds and humbles all Christians other than those who close their minds and hearts to the unique beauty of Mary, God makes Himself dependent upon the receptive heart and discerning response of the one Luke calls simply "a virgin named Mary."

---

concrete on the day of Pentecost, at the moment of the Church's birth from the Holy Spirit: Mary is in the midst of the praying community that becomes the Church thanks to the coming of the Spirit. The correspondence between Jesus' Incarnation by the power of the Spirit in Nazareth and the birth of the Church at Pentecost is unmistakable." *Mary: The Church at the Source*, 56-57.

[15] *Of Holy Virginity*, 11.

[16] St. Bernard of Clairvaux writes: "The whole world is waiting, prostrate at your feet. Not without reason, since upon your word depends the consolation of the wretched, the redemption of captives, the liberation of the condemned; in a word, the salvation of all the sons of Adam, of your whole race." *Super missus est* 4, 8; PL 183, 83D.

"The angel said to her, 'Hail, O highly favored one,
the Lord is with you!'"

Gabriel is on a mission. Like all angels, he is a "messenger" sent from God. He announces to Mary what sounds like tidings of great joy. For he comes from God's presence where all is perfect joy, perfect gladness, perfect beauty and goodness. Yet, again like all angels, he delivers his message without enthusiasm, without emotion. Angels are not emotional creatures. As St. John of the Cross reminds us, they look on human beings, especially our faults and virtues, with relative indifference.[17] They simply communicate to us what the Lord needs us to know at any given point in His providential plan. Angels are deliberately blind to motives and reasons, whether human or divine. Their words of announcement are, therefore, plain statements of fact. What may appear to be exciting news and tidings of joy to human ears – especially those disposed to hear good things about Mary – are, from the perspective of heaven, realities decreed by the Father and given in matter-of-fact form to the human persons involved.

This makes the angel Gabriel's announcement to Mary all the more important. He declares her to be God's "highly favored one." Later the Church would discern in these words the Scriptural basis for the dogma of the Immaculate Conception. In Greek (κεχαριτωμένη/*kecharitomene*) "highly favored one" means "she who

---

[17] "The soul in this transformation of love resembles the angels who judge perfectly the things that give sorrow without the feeling of sorrow, and exercise the works of mercy without the feeling of compassion…" St. John of the Cross, *Spiritual Canticle*, XX, 10.

has been perfected." The angel's statement of fact is the message that in the Father's eternal providence, Mary has already been made perfect. And, since there is no time in God, it is impious and unbecoming of us to inquire 'when' this perfecting of her was actually accomplished. Apologetics are altogether out of place when contemplating the facticity of the angel's announcement. Gabriel is decreeing an accomplished fact in the holy Wisdom of God. Mary's Immaculate Conception and resultant human perfection is a *fiat accompli* in the eternal plan of the Father's redemption. God's *fiat* regarding Mary's constitution pre-exists whatever prevenient grace she received making her His "highly favored" one. The temporal-sounding grammar of "highly favored" must not lure us into speculating about, much less wrangling over, the timing or nature of Mary's perfection in the plan of the Lord. It is a fact accomplished in the Trinity well before the foundation of the world (cf. Jn. 17:24; Eph. 1:4; 1 Pt. 1:20). The ineffability of this mystery is reflected in the matter-of-fact way the Gabriel addresses the Blessed Virgin Mary.

"Highly favored one," however, is no banal announcement. If "highly favored" means "having been perfected," then "one" means that Mary is the only one on whom this favor has been bestowed. The angel's greeting implies that there is no other "highly favored" like Mary. There is none like her. She is absolutely singular, unrepeatable. With God, of course, nothing is created merely as an instance of a wider species or genus. These are human categories imposed by fallen human intelligence on the incomprehensible diversity of the Lord's creation. There are no two snowflakes alike, no to persons the same. "Not a sparrow falls to the ground but that the Father, who made it, is unaware" (Lk. 12:6-7). The concern of the unseen God for the tiniest of His creatures is incomprehensible to the finite mind. How much more so with Mary?! "Highly favored" elevates her in the Father's eyes over all other human persons, creating, perfecting, calling, and equipping her as the one and only Mother of His only-begotten Son. When the angel announces to Mary that she is the "highly favored one," he is singling her out in an event as uniquely ingredient to God's purposes as when, at Jesus' Baptism, the Father is heard saying, "This is my beloved Son, listen to Him!" (Mk. 9:7).

As God's "highly favored one," Mary is the receiver of His ineffable grace. Everything is done *to* her to prepare her for her co-operation with His inscrutable design. She is God's gifted one. She is the recipient of His prevenient and ineluctable election. In this she resembles and fulfills Abraham and the entire people of Israel. All holiness comes from God alone. He is the Source of all holiness that redounds to human persons as a participation in His unknown and unknowable divine nature (2 Pt. 1:4). Mary enjoys this to the full, even before she is born. And she is holy in truth. The angel's description of her as "highly favored" is no legal fiction or title of imputation. God has perfected her in reality as the only worthy abode for His Son who will declare Himself the Way, the Truth, and the Life (Jn. 14:6). Mary is truly "full of grace," not as a substance filling her soul but as a transformation of her created human nature such that every fiber of her being is preserved from the deleterious effects of sin.

"The Lord is with you!" For Mary, this statement is synonymous with her title, "highly favored one." Her holiness is altogether deriv-ative of the Father's association of Mary with Himself. His choice of her to be mother of His Son is her Immaculate Conception. Nothing is given to Mary for Mary herself. Her perfection is revealed in her automatic awareness and acceptance of this fact. She knows herself in no other way than as "handmaiden of the Lord." Later we will see the full extent of her self-dispossession.

There are many ways of being "with" someone. "With" is a multivalent term. At this point in the narrative, Mary is unaware of her three-fold relationship with the Trinity: Daughter of the Father, Mother of the Son, Spouse of the Holy Spirit. She has no conception of her own Immaculate Conception. She cannot conceive of what "highly favored" could mean. Yet, her inability to conceive of the greatness of the moment - the virginal innocence of her response to Gabriel's greeting – reveals the humility of a heart pure and fertile enough to receive and conceive the Seed of Abraham, the Son of the Father.

Mary defines intimacy with God. She is in perfect union with the Lord who is "with" her. This is something said not even of the greatest prophets of the Old Testament, beginning with Moses, who encountered God face to face (cf. Gen. 32:30). Her association with the Trinity precedes and transcends human understanding. In Mary, the Father reveals that abiding with Him and His Son is a new possibility for the human race. In Mary, the Father makes known that "fear" of Him is being transformed into familiarity.

Nor must we forget the angel's command to "rejoice!". "Hail!" in many translations is rendered as "rejoice!" Joy always characterizes the saints of God. Later we will find Mary exclaiming, "...my spirit *rejoices* in God my savior!" (Lk. 1:47). Her joy consists not at all in her exultation as the Lord's "highly favored one." The Source and Object of her joy is "God my Savior." She rejoices *in Him*: it is the Holy Spirit, already united to Mary as her Spouse, who causes joy to erupt in praise of the Father. She is already abiding in the life of the Trinity more deeply than she is aware.

Wherever the Word of God arrives it arrives to save. The Son's very name – Jesus – means "Yahweh saves." Jesus does not merely bring or embody salvation. He *is* salvation in his very Person. Salvation is God. Redemption is the restoration of human communion with the triune God. It is participation in the Life of the Trinity. It is union without absorption with God whose Name, Nature, and Mission is Mercy.

Mary's joy is as ineffable and uncontainable as that found in the Trinity itself. No spoken words can adequately express its fullness, just as it's not the words of Jesus that save us but contact with Him as the Incarnate Word. Gathered around Mary, as the apostles were at Pentecost (Acts 1:14), we encounter the Living Person of the Word, the risen Jesus, in the joy and power of the Holy Spirit. The fruits of the Holy Spirit include peace and joy. A joyless Christianity is no Christianity at all. Mary's joy, even in her bewilderment, is the prototype of all those "begotten of God" (1 Jn. 5:1). Our encounter with the Word of God should always arrest us. His every interaction with us re-structures our lives, simplifying our priorities and deepening our commitment to live for Him alone. The telltale sign of our transformation in Christ is joy. For one cannot be espoused to Him, like Mary, without expressing and exhibiting the joy that wells up automatically within us when we even faintly discern the voice of our Beloved (Song 2:8, 12, 14; 8:13; cf. Rev. 3:20).

Finally, it is important to note that Gabriel's salutation to Mary is modeled closely on Zephaniah 3:14-15: "Sing aloud, O daughter Zion; shout, O Israel! Rejoice and exult with all your heart, O daughter Jerusalem! The LORD has taken away the judgments against you, he has turned away your enemies. The king of Israel, the LORD, is in your midst; you shall fear disaster no more." Pope Benedict XVI comments: "In the address of the angel the underlying motif in the Lucan portrait of Mary surfaces: she is *in person* the true Zion, towards whom hopes have yearned throughout…history. She is the true Israel *in whom* Old and New Covenant, Israel and Church are indivisibly one. She is the "people of God" bearing fruit through God's gracious power."[18] It is as if the whole of Israel's history culminated in the birth of Mary. She becomes the New Land in which the Divine Seed of the Father's Eternal Word would be planted and fertilized by the Holy Spirit. Mary is the New Mt. Zion, as well as the New Ark of the Covenant, wherein the Lord was pleased to take up His dwelling and where the Messiah and His New Law would appear.

---

[18] Joseph Cardinal Ratzinger, *Daughter Zion: Meditations on the Church's Marian Belief*, 43 (emphasis added).

*"But she was greatly troubled by his words and pon-
dered what sort of greeting this might be."*

Mary's immediate reaction is to be "greatly troubled." Some translations say "perplexed." There exists a fine line between "troubled"
and "tempted," between "difficulty" and "doubt."[19] A comparison
between Mary and Zechariah, husband of Elizabeth, is revealing.
When an angel of the Lord announced to Zechariah that he and
Elizabeth would conceive and bear a son (Lk. 1:13), he responded
with words almost identical to those of Mary. But a different spirit
reigns in his heart. He also is troubled and perplexed. Yet, his reaction is one of suspicion and doubt. He exhibits fear, mistrust, and
insecurity. Mary's reaction is just the opposite. She displays trust,
deference, and an innocent incomprehension. Her reaction is rooted
in her humility. Her bewilderment is holy, as it stems from her experience of God's purity and goodness overshadowing and transcending her own vow of virginity made as a child in the Temple. The
Light of the Son (Jesus) is already eclipsing the beauty of the moon
(Mother Mary). Her intellect is darkened, yes, even as the eyes of her
heart begin to adjust to the divine light overshadowing her. Mary
experiences a "dark night of the soul," that same experience of incomprehension that the greatest of all saints undergo, often for their
entire lives.[20] She thus experiences here an initial foretaste of the

---

[19] It was John Henry Cardinal Newman who wrote, "Ten thousand difficulties do
not make one doubt, as I understand the subject; difficulty and doubt are incommen-
surate." *Apologia Pro Vita Sua*, chapter 5, 'Position of My Mind Since 1845.'
[20] John of the Cross writes, "This contemplation, in which the soul, by means of
her transformation [divinization], has sublime knowledge in this life of the divine

troubling bewilderment and perplexing predicaments the Father will bring her into as the Mother of Sorrows and Jesus' Co-Redemptrix.[21]

Mary's "troubled" reaction to the announcement of the angel stands in illustrative contrast to other persons and entities in the New Testament. Evil spirits are "troubled" at the approach of Jesus (cf. Mk. 1:24, Lk. 4:34). Herod is "perplexed" at the silence of the Son of Man (Lk. 23:9-10). The apostles are "perplexed" at finding no body in the tomb of the Lord (Lk 24:22). Even the waters at the pool of Siloam are described as "troubled" when the angel touches them, indicting the approach of the time for healing (Jn. 5:7). Together with that of Zechariah, these other examples of being troubled or perplexed have a tenor of anxiety or dread about them. They are reactions that seem to wonder "why?". The bewilderment of Mary, however, seems to be one of wondering "how?" (Lk. 1:34). We can discern in Mary an openness to something greater than that of which she can conceive. We see in Mary an immediate receptivity to a Power greater than herself. She seems instinctively aware of the overwhelming enormity of the Father's action in the world, and she exhibits an unquestioning acceptance of a Wisdom that transcends and overshadows – dismantles and re-arranges – her inherited

---

grove and its living beauty is consequently called 'night.' Yet, however sublime this knowledge may be, it is still a dark night when compared with the beatific knowledge she ask for here." *Spiritual Canticle*, 39. 2.

[21] The notion of Mary as Co-Redemptrix seems offensive and off-putting to all but the mystics. Thus, Adrienne Von Speyr can write, "As the new Adam he [Jesus] needs the new Eve." In the Divine Economia, "Man alone should not be the one who is redeeming and redeemed: woman, too, should be the first redeemed and therefore co-redeeming. Just as Adam and Eve have sinned with one another, sh, too, must the Son and the Mother, at another level, redeem with one another; they put the work of redemption into place where the fall from sin occurred. Eve drew Adam into sin, and Christ draws Mary into redemption." (*Handmaid of the Lord*, 37, *Mary in the Redemption*, 65.) Von Speyr's thought here echoes the insight of St. Irenaeus, "the knot of Eve's disobedience was untied through the obedience of Mary. For what the virgin tied through unbelief, the Virgin Mary set free through faith (*Adversus Haereses* III, 22, 4). For a more contemporary, dogmatically legitimated version of this mystical insight, see Balthasar and Ratzinger, *Mary: The Church at the Source*, 114.

understanding of God. Being "troubled," for Mary, is a function of her unconditional trust. It reveals her instinctual deference to God in all things, even in the things dedicated to God, including her virginity. As Rene Laurentin has written, "Her fear comes not from lack of understanding or from that small-hearted anxiety to which some would like to reduce it. It comes from…that immeasurable joy which can make the most hardened natures quake."[22]

Mary also *"pondered what sort of greeting this might be."* Mary ponders many things, especially the words and actions of her Son (Lk. 2:19). She ponders these mysteries not with a critical spirit or after the manner of intellectual analysis. She ponders them rather to enter into them at a deeply personal and contemplative level. The Word of God engages her at the deepest center of her being. Nothing of God is a mere curiosity for Mary. She hears all He has to say as an invitation to taste the Trinitarian glory from whence His address comes forth.

Mary is the true contemplative. She accepts nothing at face value. She sees everything as sacramental. She sees all created things as reflecting and revealing something about God. Before Aquinas or Balthasar, Mary knew instinctively that all excellences found in the world somehow have their origin and end in the Trinitarian Mystery. None of this is conscious in Mary, of course, but the Lord is her unquestioned referent for anything and everything.

Mary is also engaged in discernment. She is feeling out the form and content of the angel's greeting. All this transpires at the level of instinct and intuition for Mary. She trusts only the light of love that shines in her heart.[23] She has no concept of her own Immaculate Conception; yet, in the purity, innocence, and naiveté of her virginal soul, Mary can conceive of what she hears only in terms of the resonances in her heart. She has nothing deeper to trust than

---

[22] Quoted in Ratzinger, *op. cit.*, 43.

[23] Like the quieted soul in St. John of the Cross' poem: "On that glad night, in secret, for no one saw me, nor did I look for anything, with no other guide than the one that burned in my heart." *Dark Night of the Soul*, Prologue, Stanzas of the Soul.

her heart-felt instincts for God. She is not one who "reflects upon" what she has heard. Instead she examines things in the light of the prayer pulsating perpetually in her heart. She is "troubled" and she "ponders." Her discernment is of a piece with her prayer. She shows us that the only true way of knowing the Will of God in any matter is through contemplative prayer, not by way of conceptual analysis. Love of God is an affair of the heart before it is a matter for the mind. In this Mary anticipates and exceeds the saints and mystics, including Sts. John of the Cross and Ignatius of Loyola, for whom "deified affectivity" and a highly refined capacity of the discernment of spirits are both the evidence and result of the truly contemplative heart.[24]

---

[24] For the importance of affectivity in discernment of God's Will, see Philip Krill, *Life in the Trinity: A Catholic Vision of Communion and Deification*, 103-120, Joseph Cardinal Ratzinger, *Behold the Pierced One*, 54-56, and Dietrich von Hildebrand's entire book, *The Heart*.

"The angel said to her, 'Do not fear, Mary, for
you have found favor with God.'"

The angel introduces an important existential component to the mystery unfolding here. Gabriel immediately discerns Mary's hesitation. Also, he uses her name for the first time. He is helping Mary take in what he, as an angel, comprehended in an instant: that God would become man, and that the maiden from Nazareth would be His mother. Gabriel is trying to put Mary's mind at ease. He is helping her begin the process of integrating who she is as "Mary" with her mission of being the pre-ordained *Theotokos* (God-bearer/ Mother of God).

Angels can tell when human beings are afraid. They cannot read our minds, but they can read our moods. As fallen, finite creatures, we are always, in some sense, teetering on the fulcrum between belief and unbelief. Angels have the power, given them by God, to insinuate thoughts and ideas into us. Both good and bad angels – Guardian Angels and demonic spirits – have the capacity to influence our thinking. Attentiveness to our thinking process, therefore, can help discern the action of good and evil spirits in our lives. Gabriel is among the best of the angels. He seeks to fill Mary's hesitation with the comfort and truth he brings from God.

Gabriel tells Mary "be not afraid!" This admonition anticipates and echoes the same consoling challenge Mary's Son will issue to His disciples. Walking on water during a storm on the sea, for example, Jesus says to his frightened apostles, "It is I, be not afraid!" (Mt. 14:27; cf. 8:26; 10:31; 17:7; 28:10). Anyone as intimate and as obedient to the Father as the good angels knows that in the service and love of God there is never any question of servile fear. "I do not call you servants any longer, because the servant does not know what the master is doing; but I have called you friends, because I have made known to you everything that I have heard from my Father" (Jn. 15:5). "Perfect love casts out fear" (1 Jn. 4:18). Fear of making a mistake, fear of doing the wrong thing, fear of abandonment: these difficulties disappear once one surrenders to and is enfolded in the Trinitarian Embrace.

There is, at the same time, a proper and holy fear of God. "The fear of the Lord is the beginning of Wisdom" (Prv. 9:10). The fear that issues in Wisdom, however, is not a heteronymous fear. It is not the terrified trepidation that pictures God as our Adversary, One whose Will and intent is to oppose our own at every turn. When the Letter to the Hebrews asserts, "It is a fearful thing to fall into the hands of the living God" (Heb. 10:31), it is describing a fear of awe and wonder, an amazement at the overwhelming majesty of God's love. It is not the fear and trepidation associated with the many false gods who inspire dread and terror in their adherents because of their blood-thirsty and insatiable hunger for human sacrifice.

All religions have imagined God as the *mysterium tremendum*: the tremendous mystery.[25] In all religions other than the one focused on Jesus, this *mysterium tremendum* is portrayed as an object of terror. The Jews themselves were not unfamiliar with this conception of God. Just to see, touch, or otherwise run afoul even of the objects consecrated by the All-Holy was to die (Ex. 19:12; cf. Gen. 3:3; Nm. 4:15). Jesus transforms the fear of God into the love of God. He reveals the Lord God as not only approachable but touchable. "We declare to you what was from the beginning, what we have heard, what we have seen with our eyes, what we have looked at and touched with our hands, concerning the word of life" (1Jn 1:1).

Peter experienced this good and holy fear when, overwhelmed

---

[25] A term and concept made famous by Rudolph Otto in his book, *The Idea of the Holy*.

17

by his shame and sense of unworthiness in the presence of Jesus' first miraculous catch of fish, declared, "Leave me, Lord, for I am a sinful man!" (Lk. 5:8). Peter, James, and John experienced this same kind of fear on Mount Tabor as they were rendered stupefied by the manifestation of the Son's Trinitarian glory (Mk. 9:6). Here they share the same experience as Moses whose many encounters with the living God left him totally humbled, yet completely transformed and equipped for his mission (Ex. 34:30-35). It is no coincidence that Moses and Elijah are speaking with Jesus at His Transfiguration (Mt. 17:3). These prophets, and all the others of the Old Covenant, were transfigured by the Spirit of God, overwhelmed and inundated by His divine fire, and prepared for their vocation by a theophany of God (e.g., Isa. 6:1-8; Ez. 2:1-4; Jer. 1:4-10). Only a serious encounter with the living God can turn the servile fear of God into the reverential and respectful fear of God that leads to Wisdom. It is one thing to experience a sense of our unworthiness in the presence of Christ's overwhelming love and compassion; it is quite another to cower in fear, terrified of "falling into the hands of an angry God."[26]

"Do not fear, Mary, you have found favor with God."

The name of "Mary" – the person of Mary – forms the link between "Do not fear" and "you have found favor with God." Mary, as mentioned earlier, means "beloved." The word "beloved," both as an adjective and a noun, finds its "incarnation," as it were in the person of Mary. The maiden of Nazareth embodies what the name and figures bearing this name in the Old Testament (Ex. 15:20; Nm. 12:1-15; 1 Chr. 4:17; Mic. 6:4) only prefigured and foreshadowed.

---

[26] The title of a famous sermon by Jonathan Edwards. Also, a description of the neurotic fear that prompted Martin Luther to seek consolation in a misappropriation of St. Paul's doctrine of justification by faith alone. See the Lutheran scholar Krister Stendahl's ground-breaking article prompting within the Protestant world what is called 'The New Perspective on Paul' called *"The Apostle Paul and the Introspective Conscience of the West."*

Mary is a player in the *economia* of salvation. She is a key and indispensable actor in the Theo-drama of redemption. The person of Mary cannot be replaced with abstract qualities nor written off as an unimportant pawn on the chessboard of God's providential end game. Following the Baptist, whose name is indivisibly linked to his unique role as Forerunner of the Messiah (Lk. 1:15-17), and who is the last of the prophets of the Old Covenant and the "greatest born of woman" (Mt. 11:11), Mary is the woman of the Apocalypse (Rev. 12:1ff.): she who gives birth to the One who "makes all things new" (Rev. 21:5). In her very person, Mary is the first and unrepeatable example of those redeemed by Christ. She is the first human being whose personal identity in Jesus can never be reduced to an example or instance of anything other than *who* – not what – they are as "new creations" in Christ. "What" someone is permanently transformed into "who" they are in Christ when He calls them by name and they respond in faith to His call (e.g. Mt. 9:9).

In Mary the Old Testament assumption that a person's name = their identity is brought to full stature. As the proto-type of all those re-created in Christ, Mary reveals that "who" we are in her Son is a singular mystery identical with the name the Lord has written for each of us on a white stone in heaven (Rev. 2:17). Our true face and our true name are identical, though hidden, in Christ (Col. 3:3). In Mary they are visible for all to see. She is – as "Mary" – the Mother of the Son, Daughter of the Father, and Spouse of the Holy Spirit. Mary = Beloved = Our Lady of the Trinity. No gap exists between Mary, her name, and her identity in God.

Mary is "beloved of God," therefore, not as one among many, nor simply as one receiving special blessings and graces from the Lord. She is "beloved of God" in very truth. "In very truth" here means that Mary is described as "beloved" in the same sense as Jesus describes Himself as "the Way, the Truth, and the Life" (Jn. 14:6). He is not an example or an instance of another, pre-existing "truth": He *is* the Truth…in very truth. "Truth" and the "Person of Jesus" are mystically the very same Mystery. Similarly, with Mary. *She defines the meaning of "beloved"* by being who she is; she is not predicated 'as beloved' by virtue of comparison to some standard outside herself. She is not considered "beloved," even, by reference to the prevenient graces received to constitute her as the Immaculate Conception. As she told St. Bernadette at Lourdes, "I *am* the Immaculate Conception," just as Jesus tells his disciples, "I *am*…the Truth" (Jn, 14:6). We see here Mary using in a derivative way the holy "I am" that applies ultimately only to God (Ex. 3:14). Yet, she uses it correctly because she is the "Highly Favored One of God" (Lk. 1:28) who at the same time "has found favor with God" (Lk. 1:30). Mary's "finding favor" with God is a function of her *being* God's Highly Favored One eternally prior to the announcement of the angel. Mary is the single person in God's divine *economia* in whom all measures of "being in favor" with God are found. Mary is literally and figuratively incomparable. All other saints and holy persons in God can be said to be such only insofar as they approximate her singular blessedness as His most "Highly Favored One."

As the incomparably Favored One who now learns from Gabriel that she has "found favor with God," Mary receives a new dimension of awareness. Mary does not need to be told – though Gabriel connects the dots – that "finding favor with God" renders fear unnecessary and irrelevant (Lk. 1:30). We know from experience that fear is driven out to the degree that we become aware of God's love for us (1 Jn. 4:18). Mary had never a doubt about God's love for her, thus she is neither surprised nor made afraid by the announcement that she "has found favor with God." Being the Highly Favored one, she has no need to "find" favor with God. Nor does she feel a need to know how, why, or in which way she has "found favor" with God. The angel says it, so it must be. Her status both as Highly Favored and "having found favor" seem, in some sense, self-evident to Mary, but without the least touch of presumption or pride. We catch a glimpse here of Mary's humility, which is of a piece with her being the Highly Favored One of God. She exhibits a calm recognition and acceptance of "what is." She is most content with matters of fact. She undertakes no analysis, no introspection. She shows immediate acceptance, interiorly free of any obstacles to ownership and integration of the mystery disclosed by the angel. If we perceive in Mary a hesitant wonderment, it is just that: amazement at the great things the Lord can do for her and others, as well as an immediate intuition of the implication for her obedient cooperation.

Mary shows us how trust and truth reciprocally reinforce each other. Faith precedes understanding, and understanding strengthens faith. Mary embodies this "hermeneutic of faith."[27] Because she trusts completely in God, the truth of her identity and mission is revealed to her. As she is told the truth about what God asks of her, she embraces it fully and her reliance upon God deepens. Interiorly she goes from surrender to surrender. In the things of God, we must believe in order to see (cf. Mk. 10:51-52). Seeing with eyes formed by faith, our trustful surrender to the triune God increases.

Mary, of course, never lacked trust in God. She never felt "out of favor" with Him such that the angel's announcement that she was His "Highly Favored One" took her totally by surprise. She was free of all self-absorption and human presumption. Evangelical notions of "eternal security" would never have entered her head.

Fundamentalist understandings of God's grace go totally haywire when severed – as they have been from the outset – from the Marian model. However devout, sectarian theories about instantaneous salvation are fundamentally misguided. Often fueled by an arcane perspective on St. Paul,[28] these notions – Gnostic at their core – confuse by conflation St. John's description of God in Christ be-

---

[27] For a profound explanation of a "hermeneutic of faith" vs. a "hermeneutic of suspicion," see Pope Benedict XVI, *Verbum Domini*, 31-39. "Benedict argues that in addition to the essential scientific study, faith is necessary for a full understanding of the texts, which in their most literal sense speak of experiences and realities that transcend human experience" (Scott Hahn, *Covenant and Communion*, 45).

[28] See above, n. 26 and below, n. 111.

stowing upon us "grace upon grace" (Jn. 1:16). Such confusion, such presumption never touched the Blessed Virgin Mary. She remained the "humble handmaid" of the Lord before, during, and after the announcement of her special place in the Son's redemptive mission. Mary is, therefore, nonplussed as she hears that she has "found favor with God." She is moved neither by disbelief nor presumption. She simply waits for the mystery to unfold. She remains open, as she always has been, to the mystical graces preparing her to receive the wondrous truths to come.

Mary has "found favor with God" not as a result of anything she has or hasn't done, but because of the predestined decision of the Trinity in her regard. The Father has created and prepared her to be the perfect "place" on earth for the advent of His only-begotten Son. She is one of a kind because He is one of a kind. All excellences attributed to Mary are determined by – and the obverse of – unfathomable truths about Jesus, the Incarnate Word. As the *Catechism of the Catholic Church* states: "What the Catholic faith believes about Mary is based on what it believes about Christ, and what it teaches about Mary illumines in turn its faith in Christ."[29] Mary has not earned her unique position in God's divine economia either because of her faith or her works. She is His "Highly Favored One" *because He wills it*. Her Immaculate Conception, her Perpetual Virginity, her indisputable status as Mother of God [not simply Mother of Christ, as Nestorius taught]: these titles of honor constitute, as it were, the underside of the glorious tapestry that is the life, death, and resurrection of the Redeemer. Everything granted to and asked of Mary finds its proper interpretation in the design of the Father for His dearly beloved Son. The final meaning of Mary – the ultimate source and term of all her titles and honorary images – is the Holy Spirit Himself, who alone penetrates the deepest things of God (1 Cor. 2:10).

---

[29] CCC, 487.

*"And now, you will conceive in your womb and bear
a Son, and you will name him Jesus."*

The economy of the angel's announcement reflects the passionate nature of God's providential *economia*. Gabriel moves forward with a certain haste in his discourse with Mary, much like Mary herself will "go in haste to the hill country of Judea" to visit Elizabeth (Lk. 1:39). He gets quickly to the heart of his announcement. It's as if he expects Mary to process the momentous content of what she is hearing as quickly as he. It may also be that he is showing us how all the graces bestowed upon Mary are for the advent of the Son whom she is informed she will conceive.

Gabriel's announcement is just that: a proclamation, not a command. He is stating what in his mind is already, in a certain sense, an accomplished fact. He is not explicitly asking Mary's consent. He is simply stating what is about to happen in history as a result of God's design from all eternity (cf. Isa. 7:14). Mary is to "conceive in your womb and bear a son." "Conceiving" and "bearing" seem to be distinct yet inseparable realities. Importantly, neither is altogether passive. Mary is a central actor in the drama of salvation that is taking place here, an epicenter of human freedom that appears paradoxical when juxtaposed with the *fiat accompli* of the angel's words.

"Conceive" connotes an element of cooperation and intentionality that is more active, say, than "receive." Mary is to "conceive" a Son in her womb, not simply to "receive" her Son from on high. Mary is no mere receptacle of the Holy Spirit in which the Eternal Word is simply deposited, indifferent, as it were, to the event of

23

salvation that is occurring within her. Any interpretation of Mary –
it bears frequent repeating! – that reduces her role in the birth, life,
death, or resurrection of Jesus to a biological or mechanical transac-
tion fundamentally distorts the Christological mystery.[30] Such views,
often fueled by an anti-Catholic polemic, obscure our perception,
not only of who Mary is in the Father's plan of redemption, but of
Jesus' identity Himself as true God and true man. The human being
who is "Jesus" is not a nondescript instance of generic humanity,
but ineluctably the 'son of Mary,' just as "Mary" is singularly and
uniquely the 'Mother of God." It is not enough, in fact, to assert
that Jesus is not God if Mary is not the Mother of God (Council
of Ephesus); we must insist further: the Lord we believe in is not
"Jesus" if His mother is not specifically the maiden from Nazareth
named "Mary." Names matter. They denote personalities that are
irreducible mysteries iconic of the Persons inseparably related in
the Trinity. The personalism involved in linking the human person
named Mary with the divine Person named – in the mystic vision of
St. Luke - Jesus transcends, and gives the lie to, all minimalist views
of Mary that fail to contemplatively comprehend her "conceiving in
her womb and bearing a son."

Mary conceived Jesus in her heart, St. Augustine tells us, before

---

[30] Hence John Henry Cardinal Newman: "…as regards the Blessed Virgin, it was
God's will that she should undertake willingly and with full understanding to be the
Mother of our Lord, and *not to be a mere passive instrument whose maternity would have no
merit and no reward.* The higher our gifts, the heavier our duties. It was no light lot to
be so intimately near to the Redeemer of men, as she experienced afterwards when
she suffered with Him. Therefore, weighing well the Angel's words before giving
her answer to them-first she asked whether so great an office would be a forfeiture
of that Virginity which she had vowed. When the Angel told her no, then, with the
full consent of a full heart, full of God's love to her and her own lowliness, she said,
"Behold the handmaid of the Lord, be it done unto me according to thy word." It was
by this consent that she became the Gate of Heaven" ("Meditations and Devotions,"
Janua Coeli, emphasis added).

24

she conceived Him in her womb.[31] Mary's body is an icon of her spirit. She is driven, interiorly, by her faith. The fire of her faith seems, almost, to attract the Father, Son, and Holy Spirit. Here we glimpse the mystery of divine initiative and human willing. Mary's faith – or anyone's, for that matter – never compels the Trinity to act. Yet, the Lord, it seems, acts most powerfully, most fruitfully in the lives of those who show great faith (e.g., Lk. 7:50). "O you of little faith," Jesus chides His disciples (Mt. 6:30; 8:26; 14:31; 16:18). In Nazareth, "he could work no miracle for want of faith among the people" (Mt. 13:58; cf. Mk. 6:6; 9:24). And the gospels are full of examples of Jesus insisting, "Go in peace, your faith has made you well " (Mk. 5:34; Lk. 7:50; 8:48). One is saved by "grace working through faith," St. Paul tells us (Eph. 2:8). Mary is the proto-type of the kind of believer envisioned by St. Paul. The unparalleled depth of her faith is the human *sine quo non* for the divine mystery of the Incarnation.

The fertility of Mary's heart, then, precedes the fruitfulness of her virginal body. Virginity and fruitfulness will ultimately be seen to be the same thing, as we enter more deeply into our contemplation of Mary's desire for the living God. Following St. Augustine, we see that Mary makes the inner chamber of her soul available to God. Seeing His Bride betrothed and receptive to Him as her Lord and Master, the Father effects a nuptial union with Mary through His Holy Spirit, enabling her to conceive His only-begotten Son. Jesus is begotten of Mary in a way virginally parallel to the way He is eternally and incomprehensibly begotten of the Father. Jesus has no earthly beginning as the only-begotten Son of the eternal Father, and He has no earthly father as the only-begotten Son of Mary.

---

[31] That is why St Augustine affirms that the Virgin "conceived in her heart before her womb" (*Discourses*, 215, 4). See also: Pope Francis, Angelus meditation for the Solemnity of the Immaculate Conception, December 8, 2014 (https://w2.vatican.va/content/francesco/en/angelus/2014/documents/papa-francesco_angelus_20141208.html)

"...you will conceive in your womb and bear a son, and you will name him Jesus."

Only a mother knows what it means to "conceive and bear a son." To "bear" is greater than "to give birth to." It is "to carry": both in the womb and forever after. A woman who is any son's mother never stops being his mother, nor he her son. It is not for nothing that many men cry out for their mothers at the moment of death. Jesus, in His own way, does something of the same (Jn. 19:26). But because He is also her Lord and Savior, Jesus sees to His mother's protection and comfort, even as a sword pierces her heart. At the moment of His greatest suffering, she will do the same for Him.

What does it mean for a mother to bear a son? We know He was perfectly obedient to her. Jesus is the perfect Son, fulfilling the Law perfectly, which calls for perfect obedience to one's mother and father (Ex. 20:12; Deut. 5:16). Jesus not only fulfills the Law, He replaces the Law in His own Person. He doesn't simply "obey"; He *is* Obedience, both vis-à-vis His Father in heaven, and in relationship with His mother on earth. Mary is the Queen Mother who, like the mother of Solomon (cf. 1 Kg. 2:18ff.), never presumes upon the largesse of the King, but nevertheless exhibits absolute confidence that He will meet whatever need she places before Him. "Do whatever He tells you," she says to the stewards at Cana (Jn. 2:5). Can these words be spoken by anyone other than a mother whose bond with, and understanding of, her Son knows no areas of doubt, difficulty, or distrust?

They say that there is no stronger earthly love than that of a mother for her children. Can't we say this is especially true of a mother's love for her *son*, especially if he is her only child? Jesus certainly takes after Mary in every way conceivable. He has her eyes, her looks, her graceful peace. He learned His prayers and other patterns of speech at her knee. She taught Him how to talk, what to say, how to behave. He took His cues about God and man from her of the unblemished soul. His compassionate glance of mercy was born, humanly speaking, from her crystal-clear vision of the good and evil in human beings. Jesus moves the way He does in the world largely because of the parenting of Mary. He imitates her gait, her élan. All His friends see His mother in Him. Do we ever stop reflecting the example given us by our mothers? Do we ever stop desiring a repeat of that first smile we received from our mothers that represents our birth into full personhood?[32]

---

[32] Balthasar makes much of the 'the mother's smile' as the event that enables the biological child to discover itself as a unique person and also to intuitively grasp that one's being as a unique person is a gift from an Other. "The little child awakens to self-consciousness through being addressed by the love of his mother. This descent of the intellect to conscious self-possession is an act of simple fullness that can only *in abstracto* be analyzed into various aspects and phases. It is not in the least possible to make it comprehensible on the basis of the formal "structure" of the intellect: sensuous "impressions" that bring into play a categorical ordering constitution that in its turn would be a function of a dynamic capacity to affirm 'Being in absolute terms' and to objectify the determinate and finite existing object that is present here. The interpretation of the mother's smiling and of her whole gift of self is the answer, awakened by her, of love to love, when the 'I' is addressed by the 'Thou'; and precisely because it is understood in the very origin that the 'Thou of the mother is not the I' of the child, but both centers move in the same ellipse of love, and because it is understood likewise in the very origin that this love is the highest good and is absolutely sufficient and that, a priori, nothing higher can be awaited beyond this, so that the fullness of reality is in principle enclosed in this 'I'-'Thou' (as in paradise) and that everything that may be experienced later as disappointment, deficiency and yearning longing is only descended from this: for this reason, everything 'I' and Thou' and the world—is lit up from this lightning flash of the origin with a ray so brilliant and whole that it also includes a disclosure of God. In the beginning was the word with which a loving "Thou" summons forth the 'I': in the act of hearing lies directly, antecedent to all reflection, the fact that one has been given the gift of the reply; the little child does not 'consider whether it will reply with love or non-love to its mother's inviting smile, for *just as the sun entices forth green growth, so does love awaken love; it is in the movement toward the 'Thou' that the 'I' becomes aware of itself. By giving itself, it experiences: I give myself. By crossing over from itself into what is other than itself, into the open world that offers it space, it experiences its freedom, its knowledge, its being as spirit*" (*Explorations in Theology, Creator Spirit*, III, 15, emphasis added). See also Balthasar, *Theo-Logic: Theological Logical Theory: Truth of God*, II, 254-256.

Our Lord's human love of His mother equals, in its own way, His divine love of His Father. He is infinitely attached and obedient to her, just as He is eternally one in mind and will with His heavenly Father. As daughter of the Father and mother of the Son, Mary shares as fully as is humanly possible in the Father-Son relationship of love that constitutes the nature of the Trinitarian Life. Her love and fidelity to her Son parallels that of her Son with His Father, and partakes in a reciprocal way in the Father's love of the Son who equally belongs to her.

"...and you will name him Jesus..."

Mary is given power and a command to name her son "Jesus." The power to name recalls the prerogative given to Adam in the Garden: "So out of the ground the Lord God formed every animal of the field and every bird of the air, and brought them to the man to see what he would call them; and whatever the man called each living creature, that was its name (Gen. 2:19). A thing's name denotes its identity. Mary is given a share in imparting to Jesus His identity as a human being. She names Him, and thus "defines" Him, with a prerogative greater than that given to any other person. Yet is it a privilege resulting from God's divine predilection. She is naming Him in accordance with the purposes of His Father, communicated to her by the angel. She is commanded to name Him "Jesus" because He will "save men and women from their sins" (Mt. 1:21; cf. Mt. 6:13; Lk. 1:71; Rev. 1:5). Mary designates her son "Jesus" as man because He is our divine Savior in the Father's plan of salvation.

Still, we must not brush too quickly past the significance of Mary's directive to name her son Jesus. It is a power and a privilege, a prerogative and imperative, that reveals just how determinative of Jesus' identity the Father desires Mary to be. If, in Scripture, simply *knowing* the name of a person gives the knower a substantial power over the person known (cf. Gen. 32:30), what must be the relationship of the person named to the one *giving* the name? Who must Jesus be for Mary, and Mary for Jesus, when it is given to her to impart to Him His human name, a name that is synonymous with His mission as Redeemer? Certainly Mary neither creates nor confirms the Savior's mission by naming Him Jesus; yet, she is issued the singular command by God to give Him His name, receiving thereby a certain claim and authority over Jesus that, by God's grace, exceeds even that of her authority as His mother. In Mary's naming of Jesus, God's Old Testament refrain, "I have called you by name…you are mine" (Isa. 43:1), is reversed and brought to an incarnational fulfillment. A share in the Father's power to name His chosen people (Gen. 35:10) and His beloved Son (Mt. 3:17; 17:5) is given to Mary. Mary is capacitated to name and claim God's only-begotten Son as her own, and to designate Him, at God's command, as the Savior of the world.

Following Mary as the perfect daughter of the Father and disciple of her Son, we are also enabled, by the power of the Holy Spirit, to name the Savior in a manner that gives us a blessed claim upon Him. Jesus becomes Mary's own as she conceives Him in faith and gives Him the name "Savior," and he becomes ours as well when, in faith, we "call upon the name of the Lord." For, "everyone who calls on the name of the Lord shall be saved" (Rom. 10:13). "If you confess with your lips that Jesus is Lord and believe in your heart that God raised him from the dead, you will be saved" (Rom 10:9). The holy name of Jesus exercises power over both God and the demons. The Father cannot withhold any good thing from those who ask in the name of His Son (Jn. 14:4; 16:23), and the demons cannot withstand the mention of the name "Jesus" (Mk. 1:24; 10:47; 16:6). The divine name contains divine power. Mary names her Son "Jesus" so we can call upon Him and be saved (Acts 2:21).

We see now the ultimate context of this and all of Mary's prerogatives. She is given "power" over Jesus as the model and means of bringing Him to us. Her obedience opens access for us to the saving power of her only-begotten Son. Mary's privilege of naming

Jesus as our Savior and exercising authority over Him as His mother makes possible and furnishes the pattern for our ownership of Him as our Redeemer and Brother. We can call upon Jesus as our brother because Mary is honored to name Him her Son. We are graced to "own the mystery"[33] because it was given to the mother to name her Master.

We also glimpse here, in distant anticipation, the Cross of Jesus Christ. We know that Jesus takes up His cross willingly and without compulsion. He is neither psychologically nor theologically pressured into it. He lovingly embraces the instrument of His own human demise. "I have a baptism with which to be baptized, and how I am constrained until it is completed!" (Lk. 12:50). "No one takes it from me, but I lay it down of my own accord. I have power to lay it down, and I have power to take it up again. I have received this command from my Father" (Jn. 10:18). Thus, it is *the freedom and love* with which Jesus assumes His cross, not the excruciating pain experienced nor the copious amounts of blood shed, that achieves our redemption. That same redemptive freedom and love are present in embryonic form here. By allowing Himself to be named and claimed by Mary – no, by insisting upon it! – Jesus reveals His inherently self-dispossessing nature, both as God and as man. For within the Trinity, Jesus is, as Eternal Word, utterly conformed to, united with - and therefore perfectly obedient to - the utterances of His Father as given in the spirations of their Holy Spirit. He *cannot not* be obedient to the Father, so united is He with the One who begets Him. Jesus has no identity other than as that of 'the Obedient One' within the

---

[33] Words of Ignaz Franz (1774) from the hymn *Holy God We Praise Thy Name*:

> Holy Father, Holy Son,
> Holy Spirit, Three we name thee;
> while in essence only One,
> undivided God we claim thee;
> and adoring bend the knee,
> while **we own the mystery.**

Life of the Trinity. This is an eternal identity that He enfleshes and exhibits in every action of His earthly existence and in every iota of the words He utters. In what Balthasar calls the 'eternal kenosis' or *'Ur-kenosis,'* we see Jesus manifesting His self-abrogating nature as God prior, even, to His Incarnation.[34] By placing Himself at the

---

[34] "On earth, the Son is obedient to the Father in the Spirit, even to his death on the Cross. This is the intelligible form of his eternal attitude to the Father who begets him, namely, that of primal obedience in willing cooperation and gratitude. True, what we have already termed the "trinitarian inversion" (Balthasar, *Theo-Drama: Theological Dramatic Theory: Dramatis Personae: Persons in Christ,* III, 123.) applies here: now, instead of breathing forth the Spirit "consubstantially" with the Father, he (as man) receives the Father's will in the Spirit; having the same Spirit within him as the Spirit of obedience. All the same it must be said that this "kenosis of obedience" ("emptying himself of the form of God": Phil 2:7) must be based on the eternal kenosis of the Divine Persons one to another: it must be *one* of the infinite aspects of eternal life. Now, however, divine obedience requires that he surrender to men as well as to God..." (Balthasar, *Theo-Drama: Theological Dramatic Theory: The Last Act,* V, 123.)

So also, Simon Oliver, "The life of God, for Balthasar, is characterized by self-dona-tion in the form of kenosis. The revelation of this self-giving is recorded in the hymn to Christ's self-emptying in the Incarnation in Philippians 2. Within the economy of salvation, this kenosis reaches its greatest intensity on Holy Saturday when God, in sovereign freedom, endures the dereliction of godlessness. Yet it is crucial for Balthasar that this kenotic moment is not an arbitrary act of God, as if the divine had suddenly become subject to godlessness in order to be fully himself (as in the thought of Jürgen Moltmann). Rather, it is suffering and dereliction which are made subject to God, and the godlessness of Holy Saturday is always the economic outworking of God's immanent and eternal kenosis. It is at this moment in the economy of salvation that it is revealed that even that which is not God is brought to be subject to God. Moreover, as Graham Ward observes, this kenosis is not christomonistic, an act confined to Christ's Incarnation and crucifixion. Rather, divine kenosis, as trinitarian and eternal, is the possibility of God's self-giving within the economy of salvation. As Aquinas refers to the eternal emanation of the Son from the Father, so for Balthasar the Father pours out his life without remainder in the Son's eternal begetting. The Son's response is kenotic eucharistia, thus constituting a "eucharistic movement back and forth from the Father." Importantly, the self-donation of the Father is also the self-reception of the Son, thus constituting the relational nature of the eternal divine gift: self-donation and self-reception are one. This love cannot be contained within an enclosed dyad, but opens in eternity in the procession of the

mercy and service of Mary – even so far as to commanding that she give Him His Name – the Lord of all sounds an overture to the way in which He will lay down His life, not only in obedience to Mary, but also for sinners like ourselves who will do not much other than buffet, abuse, and murder Him.

We can never make an end of mining the golden graces hidden and contained in the holy Name of Jesus. Our very pronunciation of the Name itself causes the cosmos to shake (cf. Rev. 6:13), the demons to shudder (Mk. 1:24), and the good angels and saints to adore (Rev. 4:10). When the angelic powers hear the saving Name of Christ they can do nothing other than repeat the refrain:

'Holy, holy, holy, the Lord God the Almighty, who was and is and is to come!" (Rev 4:8)

With them, we affirm the marvelous words of St. Paul:

"... at the name of Jesus every knee should bend, in heaven and on earth and under the earth, and every tongue

---

Spirit, who maintains the infinite difference between Father and Son. This infinite diastasis is revealed in the Son's cry of dereliction on the cross and in the silence of Holy Saturday. Within that hiatus is contained not only sin, but the whole of creation, for the "otherness" of creation—the ontological difference—is itself the *imago* of the infinite difference which is being itself, namely the difference of the divine persons. Balthasar writes, "If, within God's identity, there is an Other, who at the same time is the image of the Father and thus the archetype of all that can be created; if, within this identity, there is a Spirit, who is the free, superabundant love of the 'One' and of the 'Other,' then both the otherness of creation, which is modeled on the archetypal otherness within God, and its sheer existence, which it owes to the intra-divine liberality, are brought into a positive relationship to God." In fact, for Balthasar, it is only the difference inherent within being itself that makes creaturely difference intelligible—especially the difference within all creatures, that between essence and existence." ('Love Makes the World Go 'Round: Motion and Trinity,' In D. L. Schindler (Ed.), *Love Alone Is Credible: Hans Urs von Balthasar as Interpreter of the Catholic Tradition*, 182–184.

should confess that Jesus Christ is Lord, to the glory of God the Father" (Phil. 2:10)

Such associations from Scripture could be multiplied *ad infinitum*. Hence, perhaps the greatest of all prayers – with the possible exception of the Lord's Prayer itself – is the Jesus Prayer. As those insist who have been deified through the internal purification and spiritual transfiguration that occurs when a person is faithful to saying this prayer, "The name of our Lord Jesus Christ, descending into the depths of the heart, will subdue the serpent holding sway over the pastures of the heart, and will save our soul and bring it to life."[35] This experience issues in an admonition we do well to heed: "Abide constantly with the name of our Lord Jesus Christ, so that the heart swallows the Lord and the Lord the heart, and the two become one."[36] What a glorious treasure we have inherited, all because Mary obeyed the angel's command, *"...and you will name Him Jesus"*!

---

[35] *Writings from The Philokalia on the Prayer of the Heart*, 223.
[36] Ibid., 223.

"He will be great, and will be called the Son of the Most High; and the Lord God will give him the throne of his father David, and He will reign over the house of Jacob forever, and of his kingdom there will be no end."

Jesus' greatness is that of a Son. His greatness is that of obedient service in love and devotion. Humility is built into his identity, status, and title. His identity, status, and title is that of "Son." His very nature is that of obedient Son and Servant. He has ontological autonomy but relational subordination. Yet, his is an obedience and deference that is not compelled because it is of a piece with his identity as Son. Service, obedience, subordination, suffering love, forgiveness, even slavery (Phil. 2:6-11; cf. Rom. 6:18): these qualities are appropriate to the One who is called "Son."[37]

We glimpse here the first intimations of the source of covenantal love within the Trinity. The Son's 'greatness' within the life of the Trinity consists in His eternal identity as one inseparably bonded with the Father *as His only-begotten.* Jesus, the Son, the Eternal Word, *cannot not* be connected with the Father. He is "committed" and "covenanted" to Him. Yet, the infinite number of expectations and "demands" of this relationship are never forced or imposed upon the Son from outside because there is no "outside" the Father-Son relationship. The Father and Son, in their greatness, *define* freedom, love, and commitment as it is understood outside their Trinitarian

---

[37] Speaking in this regard about Jesus, John Howard Yoder says, "These three strands join in one holistic, Christological, paradigmatic proclamation [of the Son]: *servanthood, enemy love, forgiveness.* If we are interested in making sense to our unbelieving or otherwise believing neighbors, let this threefold cord be the test case." *John Howard Yoder: Spiritual Writings*, 62 (emphasis added).

communion. The source of all excellences in the world – the source of all forms of love, connection, bonding, relating, and interacting – including all the covenants of the Old Testament – are found in the asymmetrical but inseparable relationship of the Son and His Most High Father.

The Trinity is revealed as soon as the angel as says Jesus is to be called "Son of the Most High." The Most High God is the Father. God the Father is the trinitarian Person traditionally designated by the generic term "God." This impersonal referent reflects the Father's essential incomprehensibility and unknowability. It also implies His unapproachability and inaccessibility apart from the incarnation of His Son. "No one knows the Father except the Son, and no one knows the Son except the Father, and those to whom the Father chooses to reveal Him (Mt 11:27). The Father is untouchable apart from contact with the Son. Jesus comes to take us to the Father (Jn. 14:3; 17:24). "We have seen him…we have touched him….we have put our very hands into his wounds (cf. Lk. 6:16; Jn. 1:14; 20:27). Indeed, through the Eucharist, we have taken him into our very being. Yet, it is not we who have chosen to assimilate him; it is he, who, loving us first (1 Jn. 4:19), chose to receive us into himself, and to bring us into His consubstantial relationship with "the Most High God," His Father (Jn. 15:16; 17:11, 21-22).

Jesus is "great" because he is the "Son" of the "Most High God." His greatness is a function of his being the Only-begotten of the Divine Monarch. This greatness expresses itself in incarnational humility, reflecting its origin in the Father's inexpressible transcendence. Jesus is the Suffering Servant among men and women because He knows Himself to be the beloved Son of the Most High Father. His humility on earth stems from and images forth His adoration and bottomless appreciation for His Father. Thus, Jesus' "greatness" is a function of being "Son"; he is *called* "great" because many recognize in Him – though " as through a glass darkly" (1 Cor. 13:12) – the Trinitarian source of His divine humility.

Our view of Jesus is always inverted when we attribute to Him titles based on epistemic criteria other than His relationship with His Father. We tend to acclaim Him as God because of qualities of "greatness" we perceive in Him as a man. But things come into proper focus only when our vision of Him *begins in the Trinity.* It is His Trinitarian glory that filters through his humble humanity and manifest itself in His words and work. This is especially the case in His Paschal suffering and death. It is His identity as Son of the Most High Father that generates the love and admiration we feel for Him. His assimilated human nature puts on visible display the ineffable love that He has for His Father. Only His Holy Spirit can enlighten us regarding the Trinitarian source of what touches us in Christ. The beginning and end of the greatness we attribute to Jesus is the ineffable union of love He enjoys with His Father.

"…and the Lord God will give him the throne of his father David…"

Jesus is Lord and God of his father, David. Jesus is descended from David in his humanity, but David's fatherhood and kingship finds its source in the Son's divinity. David is Jesus' father in terms of human kinship; Jesus is David's Father and Lord in terms of the Trinitarian economy (Isa. 9:6). It is this reality that enables Jesus to tell his disciples: 'How can the scribes say that the Messiah is the son of David? David himself, by the Holy Spirit, declared, 'The Lord said to my Lord, 'Sit at my right hand, until I put your enemies under your feet.'" (Mk. 12:36). Also in the psalms we hear David saying, "The LORD says to my lord, 'Sit at my right hand until I make your enemies your footstool'" (Ps. 110:1). David is here giving homage to the Messiah, proclaiming in advance Christ's Resurrection and Ascension and the recapitulation of all things in Him. In making this prophecy, David receives a kind of prevenient grace to "confess with his lips and believe in his heart" that Jesus is Lord (Rom. 10:9), thereby being "saved in hope" (Rom. 8:24) by the very Lord who is his descendent according to the flesh.[38]

We see also here how the Father delivers all things into the hands of His Son (Jn. 3:35). "The Father gives the redemption of the world to the Son, and the Son accomplishes it."[39] The unconditional promises in the covenant with David are grounded in the unity of the Father and Son in the Trinity. More particularly, they flow from the unrestricted deliverance of all the Father is and has to His beloved Son. The Father is the unoriginate Giver, and the Son is the ever-beholden Receiver within the trinitarian Communion. In this regard, the unilateral and unconditional covenants made with Abraham (cf. Gen. 26:4) and David (2 Sam. 7:13-16) more clearly reveal the Father's role in the economy of salvation than the more contingent and bi-lateral agreements made by Him with Adam (cf. Gen. 3:3) and Moses (cf. Deut. 11:26-28). The promises regarding the inviolability of the "throne of David" unto perpetuity derive from the infinitely unrestrained and ever-erupting love of the Father for His only-begotten Son.

Jesus' fidelity to His Father, as evidenced on the Cross (Lk. 23:46), as well as in His adoration (Mt. 11:25) and intercession (Jn. 17:9-10), makes up for and "redeems" the inconsistent ebb and flow of sin and repentance that characterized all the other standard-bearers of the covenant from Adam to Abraham and from Moses to David. Jesus Himself is the fulfillment of the covenant made with David. In His perfect righteousness as the ever Faithful One on Calvary, but more primordially as the perfectly Obedient One within the Life of the Trinity, Jesus is the One who is "worthy to receive glory and honor and power" (Rev. 4:11). The "throne of his father David" that God the Father gives to His Christ is the sign in the *Economia* that Jesus, His dearly beloved Son, is not only Messiah of the Jews, but Redeemer of the world and King of all creation (cf.

---

[38] See Benedict XVI's beautiful encyclical, *Spe Salvi.*

[39] Von Speyr, *Mary in the Redemption,* 85.

1Tim. 6:15; Rev. 17:14; 19:16). The Son's reign and inheritance is *cosmic* because His relationship to His Father is even more unfathomable. The Father gives the Son the "throne of his father David" as an historical token of Jesus' intimate and immanent bond with Him in the Divine Embrace from all eternity.

"…and he will reign over the house of Jacob forever; and of his Kingdom there will be no end."

Jesus will "reign over the house of Jacob." Jacob is the wounded one. He is the one who came up lame after wrestling with God as with an angel (Gen. 32:24). Jacob is an image of wounded humanity, the collective lameness that evokes compassion in the eyes of the Lord (e.g., Mt. 11:5; 15:30-31).

Jesus collects wounded humanity into the Holy House of His Divine Temple. Jesus is that Temple (Mt. 26:61), planted firmly atop Zion and Golgotha, the Holy Mountain of the Lord, to Whom all nations are prophesied to stream: "On that day, says the LORD, I will assemble the lame and gather those who have been driven away, and those whom I have afflicted. The lame I will make the remnant, and those who were cast off, a strong nation; and the LORD will reign over them in Mount Zion now and for evermore" (Mic 4:7; cf Isa. 2:1-3). Jesus brings the corporate Jacob to Himself. He gathers them in in order to "gather them up" into His hypostatic union with His Father and the Holy Spirit (cf. Lk. 13:34).[40] We are included in Jacob. We are his wounded members, lame from our birth, permitted to be so by the Father to put on display the glory of the New Jacob, Jesus – the divinely Wounded One – who heals us.

"…and of his Kingdom (reign) there will be no end."

Luke alludes here to the prophecy of Daniel:

---

[40] See Steenberg, *God and Man*, 94 for Tertullian's use of "gather in" to connote deification in Christ.

Behold, I saw, as in a vision, one like a son of man, coming with the clouds of heaven, and he came to the Ancient of Days and was presented before him. And to him was given dominion and glory and kingdom, that all peoples, nations, and languages should serve him; his dominion is an everlasting dominion, which shall not pass away, and his kingdom one that shall not be destroyed" (Dan. 7:13-14).

Jesus inherits a kingdom. He receives it from His Father (the Ancient of Days). It is presented to Him – just as He is presented before the Father – by the elusive and invisible Holy Spirit. The kingdom is Trinitarian both in form and origin. Indeed, the Kingdom of God is nothing other than the Trinity itself, with the Son of Man on a divinely appointed mission to incorporate us into it. This is the reason the kingdom is "without end." The Trinity has no beginning or end. Jesus himself *is* the Beginning and End, the Alpha and Omega (). Jesus, as the Son of Man, is the incarnation of the Kingdom of God, given to Mary by the Holy Spirit. After the completion of His redemptive mission He is re-presented to the Ancient of Days by that same Holy Spirit, but now together with "all peoples and nations" whom He has gathered into glorious and intimate union and service with Him. The Son of God comes to earth as the Son of Man in order to deliver fallen and sinful humanity back into indestructible and irreversible communion with His eternal Father.

Jesus is a King and the entire cosmos is His Kingdom. "Dominion" and "reign" are the only appropriate ways of describing His influence over us. Yes, He is a King who serves His subjects (Mk. 10:45). He is a Suffering Servant who washes their feet (Jn. 13:14-15). He is also a King who remains silent before His detractors (Mt. 27:14), and "opens not His mouth" (cf. Isa. 57:3), even as He lovingly approaches – and embraces – His own execution (cf. Lk. 12:50; Lk. 10:18). But His words – those of a Lion (Rev. 5:5), those of a King (cf. 1 Tim. 6:15) – "burn within our hearts" (Lk. 24:32) because they issue forth from the mouth of One whose Word is larger and louder than all the oceans and hills He has created (cf.

Col. 1:17). Reverence, gratitude, and humility are, ultimately, the only appropriate demeanor when we approach the King of Kings and the Lord of lords (1 Tim. 6:15). We must divest ourselves of our pride every time we enter the Presence of Jesus Christ the King.

It is a Catholic instinct in this regard to look first to the face of Mary before gazing into the eyes of the Redeemer. Neither presumption nor despair has any place in our posture before God's only Son. For the Lord "casts down the proud but raises up the lowly" (Lk. 1:52). Our lowliness must be that of the Virgin Mother. She hardly dared to raise her eyes to the angel, not out of servile fear, but out of consummate reverence for the things of God. Like her, we must experience in ourselves our status as "not God," and express in our every action and demeanor His kingly dominion over us.[41] Mary is the Queen Mother. She does not use her status as His "highly favored one" to eliminate the distance that separates her as His creature from Him as her God. To presume upon Christ in ways that even some Protestants describe as trading in "cheap grace"[42] is to obscure and demean His kingship in our lives. Mary is forever our model in knowing how to love Jesus, her Son.

---

[41] Balthasar emphasizes the radical Otherness of God from all created being by citing Meister Eckhart's contention that "If God is Being, Not-God is Non-Being. 'All creatures are pure nothing. I am not saying that they are of little value or really something after all. They are pure nothing.' And here is the proof: 'Add the whole world to God, and you have no more than if you had God alone.'" (*The Glory of the Lord, a Theological Aesthetics: Theology: The New Covenant*, V, 42, quoting Eckhart **Sermons** 4, G I 69–70; *cf. In Exod.* 15 n. 40, L II 45)

[42] A phrase made famous by Dietrich Bonhoffer in his book, *The Cost of Discipleship*: "Cheap grace is the grace we bestow on ourselves. Cheap grace is the preaching of forgiveness without requiring repentance, baptism without church discipline, Communion without confession...Cheap grace is grace without discipleship, grace without the cross, grace without Jesus Christ, living and incarnate."

$\mathcal{L}$uke 1:34

"Mary said to the angel, 'How can this be since I am a virgin?'"

It would be easy to misread Mary's question in any number of ways. We might think she is questioning, by way of anticipation, the mechanics of the Virgin Birth. We might think she is defensively protecting the virginity which she made as a vow to the Lord. We might even think she is testing the angel to see if he is really an angel of light, since Mary is convinced that her self-surrender to God in an offering of nuptial virginity was inspired by God and that only an angel of darkness would tempt her to forego her vow of virginity in order to conceive a child. But none of these interpretations would go to the heart of Mary's question, nor to the center of Mary's virginal heart. Mary is actually soliciting Gabriel's assistance. She is seeking to grasp, and be grasped by, what she clearly recognizes as both a gift and a task from God. "Help me understand," she is asking of the angel, "how I can give myself over to God's plan for my life that exceeds even the offering of myself to Him as His consecrated virgin."

In her virginal innocence, and with the angel's assistance, Mary is beginning to see that what God has in mind for her both transcends and perfects the total self-offering she has already made of herself to Him. He is expanding her understanding of what He desires for her, and what He desires to do in, with and through her. Her virginal body will bear in the flesh the Eternal Word of God whom she has already conceived in her heart. Mary is starting to see that God is much greater, and her virginity more fruitful, than even she, in her previous piety, had imagined. She is bedazzled by the initial scope and force of the angel's announcement. Yet, she does not

41

disbelieve. It simply takes her a moment to begin to comprehend the ever-greater power and promise of the ever-exceeding Lord. Mary is the quintessentially perfect example of the believer in whom 'faith seeks understanding' (*fides quaerens intellectum*).

How different is the response of Zechariah, whose encounter with the angel Gabriel parallels that of Mary, but illustrates the exact opposite disposition (cf. Lk. 1:18). Zechariah is also promised he will receive a son whose name will be great in Israel. This son "will be filled with the Holy Spirit, …[and] turn many of the sons of Isarel to the Lord their God, going before the Lord in the power and spirit of Elijah…" (Lk. 16). Later, Jesus will say of John the Baptist, "…among those born of women no one is greater than John…" (Lk. 7:28). Yet, Zechariah is incredulous. He doesn't believe it. Worse, he masks his disbelief with an apparently harmless, seemingly appropriate question: "How shall I know this? For I am an old man, and my wife is advanced in years" (Lk. 1:18). Here we catch the sound of Sarah's laughter when, at the very beginning of God's election of Israel, she doubted the angel, whereas her husband, Abraham, never doubted (Gen. 18:1-15; 22:1-18). Zechariah follows in the same skeptical footsteps of Sarah, whereas Mary completes the pure faith of Abraham who, as Scripture assures us, "was regarded [reckoned] as righteous because of his faith" (Rom. 4:9; cf. Rom. 4:13, 16; Gal. 3:8, 14; Heb. 11:8, 17; Gen. 18:12).

There is a universe of difference separating Mary (and all those pious souls whose faith 'seeks understanding') and Zechariah (and that legion of skeptical and suspicious 'disciples' who 'hold the outward form of godliness but deny its inner power') (2 Tim. 3:5). Mary's and Zechariah's questions to the angel appear to be identical but they are as opposite as high noon and midnight. Their similarity masks the seriousness of their difference. Mary's response is the epitome and perfection of faith; Zechariah's, by contrast, is the dissimulation of doubt. Mary exhibits the most highly refined yet humble discernment of spirits, whereas Zechariah attempts to disguise his doubt with the Gnostic ruse of feigned sincerity.

Purity of faith is always virginal in character. It is totally without guile (cf. Jn. 1:47), but it is also not without discernment (cf. 1 Jn. 4:1). It is no coincidence that those who are barren but who exhibit the most exemplary faith – Abraham (cf. Gen. 18:11), Hannah (1 Sam. 1:5), Mary - are chosen by God to be most fruitful through the progeny given to them. Mary's virginity, in particular, is a function of the purity of her faith, not vice versa. She conceived Jesus in her heart, as St. Augustine tells us, long before she conceived Him in her womb.[43] Mary *is* the Immaculate Conception because *everything* she conceives of is conceived of in an immaculate and virginal way. She believes ill of no one. She thinks ill of no one. She anticipates and perfects St. Paul's admonition: "Finally, beloved, whatever is true, whatever is honorable, whatever is just, whatever is pure, whatever is pleasing, whatever is commendable, if there is any excellence and if there is anything worthy of praise, think about these things" (Phl. 4:8).

Purity is the virtue closest to God. Purity and humility are identical in Mary. The gift of her physical virginity to God is so acceptable to Him because it is offered by a heart even more primordially pure. In this Mary anticipates and fulfills the truth of what her Son taught: "The good person out of the good treasure of the heart produces good, and the evil person out of evil treasure produces evil; for it is out of the abundance of the heart that the mouth speaks" (Lk. 6:45).

A final parallel suggests itself as we contemplate Mary's questioning of the angel. This time the parallel is with Eve. "Whereas Eve asked no questions of the Serpent and was foolishly deceived through her passions by that tempter, Mary…interrogated her angelic visitor…the mother of Jesus exercised her freedom and made her choice to bear the Son of God with total sobriety."[44] Again we

---

[43] St Augustine affirms that the Virgin "conceived in her heart before her womb" (*Discourses*, 215, 4).

[44] Vigen Guroian, *The Melody of Faith: Theology in an Orthodox Key*, 67.

discern the purity of heart with which Mary assents to the invitation from God to be the Mother of His Son. But it is a purity of heart that includes a clarity of mind and an unsullied intuition. It is the perfect integration of *fides et ratio*. It avoids the instinctualism of Eve, on the one hand, and the intellectualism of Zechariah, on the other. It is neither impulsive nor elitist. Despite her tender age, Mary is a model of self-possession. This quasi-divine synergy of discernment without doubt, of faith without fideism, is given to Mary in unparalleled abundance because of her special mission conceived by God as His Immaculate Conception. Hence, Mary is called the Second Eve, "redeeming" and reversing the impassioned and disobedient disbelief of our original mother in the flesh.[45] Her obedience is so salvific[46] because it issues not from the compulsion of a fearful heart but from an epicenter of freedom, integrity and an unfettered love of God that can only be described as perfectly immaculate.

---

[45] St. Irenaeus, *Proof of the Apostolic Preaching*, 33, 69.

[46] "Mary is the *cause* of our salvation," so St. Irenaeus, *Against Heresies*, III.22.4.

"The angel said to her, 'The Holy Spirit will come upon you,
and the power of the Most High will overshadow you...'"

The Holy Spirit is "the power of the Most High." He communicates the incomprehensible, creative love of the Father to the world. The Incarnation is, from start to finish, a Trinitarian event.

It is this same Holy Spirit who "comes upon" Mary. When He first "came upon" the world, the Holy Spirit found that "the earth was a formless void and darkness covered the face of the deep..." (Gen. 1:2). Mary is now the deep, formless void He encounters, enveloped as she is in the darkness of anonymity, humility, and self-effacement, as He comes from the Father to recreate the human race. He "moves over the waters" of Mary's fluid and receptive heart, finding there an ocean of love void of any currents or waves other than the desire to serve and please God.

Because of her deep humility, it is as if the Holy Spirit is actually "drawn" to Mary. It is as if the pre-redemption of her by the Father through the Son attracts the Holy Spirit. It is as if God the Father, having arranged Mary's Immaculate Conception for His Son, now arranges a marriage for His Holy Spirit with the mother of the Son. The Father, it seems, is behind these re-creative nuptials. He sends His Holy Spirit "in the beginning" to create the world for His Son. Now He sends His Holy Spirit once more for its-recreation in Christ. Instead of a "formless void" as "in the beginning," the Holy Spirit now finds "a virgin named Mary" and He takes her for His own. It is through the power of her divine Spouse – the Holy Spirit – that Mary will become in truth the Mother of God. This enables us to forever honor her as Our Lady of the Trinity: Daughter of the Father, Mother of the Son, Spouse of the Holy Spirit.

"...and the power of the Most High will overshadow you..."

The Annunciation recalls the Transfiguration. "While he was still speaking, suddenly a bright cloud overshadowed them, and from the cloud a voice said, 'This is my Son, the Beloved; with him I am well pleased; listen to him!'" (Mt. 17:5). Like the Annunciation, the Transfiguration is a thoroughly Trinitarian event. Father, Son, and Holy Spirit are all palpably present. The Holy Spirit is the enveloping space – the Cloud of Mystery – in which the Son is seen, and the Father heard, in their divine identities. Outside the overshadowing inspiration of the Holy Spirit, neither the Son can be understood, nor the Father love and appreciated, as is worthy of them.

Mary is the perfection and fulfillment, purpose and finality, of the previous theophanies in Israel's history. She is the single virginal person – the Holy Ground from which a "stem from the root of Jesse" would sprout (Isa. 11:10; cf. Rom. 5:12). She is the Daughter of Zion for which, and to which, all former manifestations of the Glory of the Lord were pointing. She is overshadowed and protected by her spouse, the Holy Spirit, just as YHWH's beloved Israel was protected, preserved and purified by the Cloud of His Spirit as she journeyed towards the Promised Land. Mary is also the Burning Bush, engulfed in flaming love for the Lord, but never consumed (Ex. 3:2). Mary is Mt. Sinai, upon whom the Cloud descends and God's Law is perfectly received (Ex. 24:15ff.). Mary is the fertile ground, the fruitful womb, in which both the Word of God and the seed of Abraham come to full fruition (cf. Rom. 4:13). Mary is the Promised Land from whom the Messiah arises and in whom the Chosen People are meant to take refuge. Mary is the New Tabernacle (Ex. 25:9), the New Ark of the Covenant (Ex. 25:21), and the Final Holy of Holies (Ex. 26:33) upon whom the Spirit of God descends and in whom the Son of God indwells. The mist of the Shekinah disappears as the Son of Man comes forth. Jesus takes up His dwelling in womb of Mary, completing the purpose of all the preliminary locations in Israel wherein the Presence of God was believed to abide.

Mary is also enveloped by the Holy Spirit in her contemplation of her Son. She is continually in His presence as before a perpetual Epiphany of God. To be sure, His Incarnation is a *kenosis* (self-effacement). Like the apostles on Tabor, when she looks up she "sees only Jesus" (Mk. 9:8). Yet, in her spirit, Mary always discerns His divinity. She worships Him as God even when she is teaching Him to tie his sandals.

Who can approach the contemplation of Mary? Who can comprehend her mystical intuitions? She is "overshadowed" by the Holy Spirit, not only at the moment of His conception, but at every moment of her interaction with Him. The Spirit's "overshadowing" is darkest on Calvary. But, "light comes with the dawn." The Mother of Sorrows goes into the tomb with her Son. But in the Holy Redeemer, the tomb becomes a womb of rebirth. This new "womb of salvation" is now implanted in the heart of Mary. She becomes Mother of the Church, leading us to the tomb and womb of our rebirth in our Mother the Church.

"...therefore the child to be born will be holy;
he will be called Son of God"

Jesus defines holiness. "...the child to be born will *be* holy..."
Holiness is a function of Jesus, not vice versa. Jesus does not partake of a pre-existent quality of holiness; he constitutes it in his very
Person. He defines it. He *is* it. Any other created thing or person
legitimately called "holy" participates, in some shape, manner, or
form, in the Person of Jesus. "Apart from me you can do nothing,"
says the Lord (Jn. 15:5). Translation: "Apart from me nothing is
good, nothing is holy." "He is," as the Apostle says, "before all else
that is" (Col. 1:17). This includes all holy people and all holy things.

Jesus also defines holiness as "becoming childlike." "Unless
you become as a little child," he says much later, "you cannot enter the kingdom of God" (Mt. 18:3). Coming into the world as an
infant, Jesus sanctifies childlikeness as the essence and template of
holiness. Holiness = Innocence = Jesus. "Like a lamb dumb before
its shearers, led without objection to the slaughter" (cf. Isa. 53:7), so
does Jesus identify holiness with the unsuspecting and unsuspicious,
innocent beauty of the uncomprehending child. Jesus recognizes
His holiness in others also, as He says of Nathaniel, "Behold, an
Israelite in whom there is no guile!" (Jn. 1:47). Jesus Himself is the
only Guileless One. And, everyone who is "holy" participates in
some fashion in the guilelessness of the Child Redeemer.

Holiness is also power, but power now defined by the Divine
Child as weakness. "This child," Simeon tells his mother, Mary,
is "set apart" – another definition of holiness – "for the rise and

fall of many in Israel" (Lk. 2:34). Even as an innocent child, Jesus causes tumult and rebellion for the terrestrial and celestial powers that oppose Him and His Kingdom. Herod takes up arms against the child who would be King (Mt. 2:2; cf. Jn. 18:37). Satan and his minions are also disturbed when the child Jesus is born into the world (cf. Eph. 3:10). As an infant in the manger, Jesus is already bringing judgment upon the world. He is already the Prince of Peace causing the Prince of Darkness to prepare his subjects for war. Even as a child he is the light of the world, darkening the vision of those who will oppose Him (cf. Jn. 9:41). Here He is exercising a power in weakness – bound as He is in swaddling clothes upon the wood of the manger - that will be fully displayed in His death on the wood of the Cross.

This child will also *"be called Son of God."* "Son" is a purely relational term. It defines an intrinsically "beholden" identity. Jesus is the Father's "begotten," and therefore, "beholden" One. Yet, there is nothing "lacking" or "less than" in Jesus' identity or experience as the Father's only-begotten Son. "Begotten," "beholden," and "beloved" are synonymous in the *Hypostasis* of the Second Person of the Trinity. There is no heteronomy in the Trinitarian Communion. The Son has no shred of resentment in His identity as "of" and "from" the Father. He experiences Himself eucharistically (gratefully) as "to" and "for" the Father precisely because He "comes from" the Father (Jn. 8:38; cf. Jn. 3:13; 8:23; 19:11). His nature and attitude is one of eternal gratitude. He is Giving personified because He knows Himself as freely begotten of the Father and forever beloved of Him.

Since "beloved" and "beholden" are identical in the Word of God (Jesus), obedience and love are also indistinguishable in Him. Because of His derivative relationship as the only-begotten of the Father, Jesus hunger and thirst is to "do the will of my Father in heaven" (Jn. 4:34). When He says – in His Passion – "Thy will, not mine, be done!" (Mt. 26:39), Jesus is not engaged in stoic resignation to an arbitrarily gruesome fate incomprehensibly imposed upon Him by a vindictive Monarch. On the contrary, as loving Son, Christ is acceding to what, in His divine love, He perhaps conceives of as a negligible sacrificial expression (the Cross) to satisfy His Father's desire for the salvation of the world. Left to Himself, the Redeemer may well have conceived of an even more graphic or extravagant expression of His willingness to exceed the wishes of His Father in heaven. The Atonement, from a truly Trinitarian perspective, is not about "making satisfaction" in any juridical or forensic sense. Rather, it is about the Son and the Father wanting both to outdo and yet restrain (out of mutual respect) their expressions of (1) love for each other, and (2) their subsequent love of Adam and Eve, created in their image and likeness (Gen. 1:26). In no way does the tragedy and fall of sinful humanity precondition, much less cause or provoke, the theo-drama that is Christ's life on earth of pleasing His Father that culminates in his final act of self-emptying upon Calvary's gibbet. Coarse and frankly sadistic theories of Satisfaction – projections of humanity's sin upon the Principal Actors (Father, Son, and Holy Spirit) in the narrative of salvation – have made it virtually impossible to perceive the *love* in the Agony and Death of Jesus. The Light of Redemption, manifesting itself to human intellect as darkness on Golgotha, is further obscured by imaging Jesus' obedience to His Father as oppositional as our own. Jesus runs towards His Passion (cf. Lk. 9:51-53) – thirsts for "the baptism with which I must be baptized" (Lk. 12:50), "takes up" and figuratively kisses His Cross – as the divinely appointed means of consummating His mission from His Father. Not only are obedience and love indistinguishable in Christ, so also are life and death. For it is only in Him who is "the Resurrection and the Life" (Jn. 11:25) that dying is made identical with coming to life in the eternal life of the Son (cf. Jn. 17:3; 6:40).

As Son Jesus is a "medial" person. The "from" and "for" that constitutes His identity as Son and Eternal Word47 originate and are anchored in His obedient and reverential (adoring) relationship with His Father, but does not remain locked up in the immanent Trinity.

Jesus is also the Son "given to us" (Isa. 9:5). This we see most pow-erfully, and most mystically, in His words, "This is my body, given for you," issued at the Last Supper (Lk. 22:19). "Unto us a child is born, unto us a child is given" (Isa. 9:6). In conceiving Jesus, Mary receives the One given "to" and "for" us all. He is the supreme gift to us from the mercy and the love of the Father.

Every scintilla of Jesus' existence as man is an image and icon of His love for His Father, turned now towards us. Just as He is 'turned towards His Father' in obedience under the inspiration of the Holy Spirit, He is not 'turned towards' us with the same love and solicitude. In and through Mary, the Son of God becomes the Son of Man. As "one like us in all things but sin" (Heb. 4:15), the Eternal Word-made-flesh reverses and completes the downward thrust of His obedience to His Father. He now lifts us up to the Father with the same love as man that He brings with Him from the Father. He goes "from" us "to" the Father, making intercession "for" us, just as He was commissioned to do by the Father (cf. Jn. 17:9). The upwards relationality of His identity as man finds its final expression in His high priestly prayer uttered on the eve of His Great Sacrifice on our behalf: "...that they may all be one. As you, Father, are in me and I am in you, may they also be in us... as we are one, I in them and you in me, that they may become completely one, so that the world may know that you have sent me and have loved them even as you have loved me" (Jn. 17:21-23). He loves us "to the end" (Jn. 13:1) in a way that parallels and derives from His love of the Father "from the beginning" (Jn. 1:1).

Whenever we gaze upon the countenance of Jesus we see a hologram of God. He reveals the Face of the Father to us, and, in the same glance, shows unto the Father the perfect face of man: the Face of the New Adam, the whole human race, fully recapitulated and restored in and through His obedient Sacrifice on the Cross.

Jesus is also the *Pontifex Max*: the perfect Bridge between God and man. He is our connection between heaven and earth, and the

Father's ladder of salvation promised to the Patriarchs. Upon His very Person "the angels ascend and descend" (Gen. 28:12). He brings God to us as Emmanuel in His Incarnation, and He brings our flesh unto the Father, deified and redeemed in Himself, imparting to us a share in the glory He "had with His Father from the beginning" (Jn. 17:5). Jesus is *Son of God* by nature, we by participation in Him.[47]

---

[47] For the patristic teaching on deification as participation in the Sonship of Jesus, see Irenaeus, *Against Heresies*, III,19,1 (SC 211, p. 374); Athanasius, *On the Incarnation*, 54:3 (PG 25, 192B) Maximus the Confessor, *Theological and Economic Chapters*, PG,90,1165; Gregory Nazianzus, *Third Theological Oration*, 19-20 (PG 36,537-38). See also, *Catechism of the Catholic Church* #460. The Scriptural root of this doctrine of deification is 1 Pt. 2:4, "partakers of the divine nature."

"Then Mary said, 'Here am I, the servant of the Lord; let it be with me according to your word.' Then the angel departed from her."

[handwritten: Already with God — not afar - not distant - Maybe not knowing, but Present - ready]

Mary's first words of response – "Here am I..." - recall and complete those of our father in the faith (Rom. 4:16), Abraham, at his moment of his greatest trial (Gen. 22:1-19). Three times in the twenty-second chapter of Genesis (22:1, 8, 11), Abraham exhibits the readiness for total love and complete surrender that the Lord desires from His chosen people and which finds consummate perfection in the *fiat* of Mary. "After these things God tested Abraham, and said to him, 'Abraham!' And he said, 'Here am I'" (Gen. 22:1). How often this response of openness and acquiescence has echoed down through the ages on the lips and in the hearts of those who love and trust God completely!

We think not only of Abraham but also of Jacob: "Then the angel of God said to me in the dream, 'Jacob,' and I said, 'Here I am'" (Gen. 31:11). God also "spoke to Israel in visions of the night, and said, 'Jacob, Jacob.' And he said, 'Here I am' (Gen. 46:2). Jacob was as eager and willing to respond to the call of the Lord as was his grandfather, Abraham, the Fountainhead of all who would believe.

Moses too is "reckoned as righteous" because of His willing response to the call of the Lord. His encounter with YHWH in the theophany of the Burning Bush is an iconic anticipation of the Blessed Virgin Mary responding in faith to the angel Gabriel:

"Moses was keeping the flock of his father-in-law Jethro, the priest of Midian; he led his flock beyond the wilderness, and came to Horeb, the mountain

of God. There the angel of the LORD appeared to him in a flame of fire out of a bush; he looked, and the bush was blazing, yet it was not consumed. Then Moses said, 'I must turn aside and look at this great sight, and see why the bush is not burned up.'

"When the LORD saw that he had turned aside to see, God called to him out of the bush, 'Moses, Moses!' And he said, 'Here I am.' Then he said, 'Come no closer! Remove the sandals from your feet, for the place on which you are standing is holy ground.' He said further, 'I am the God of your father, the God of Abraham, the God of Isaac, and the God of Jacob.' And Moses hid his face, for he was afraid to look at God. Then the LORD said, 'I have observed the misery of my people who are in Egypt; I have heard their cry on account of their taskmasters. Indeed, I know their sufferings, and I have come down to deliver them from the Egyptians, and to bring them up out of that land to a good and broad land, a land flowing with milk and honey…" (Ex. 3:1-8).

Moses is chosen as the instrument of Israel's deliverance from slavery. His readiness to respond, "Here am I!," anticipates in a beautiful way the consummate cooperation embodied in Mary's *Fiat*.

In responding to the angel, therefore, Mary speaks as the culmination of an entire lineage of pre-Christian saints whose *"Here am I"* epitomizes the faith of Israel. From Abraham to Jacob; from Moses to Samuel (1 Sam. 3:4); from Esther (Esther 14:3) to David (Ps. 40:7); from Isaiah (Isa. 6:8; 52:5-6) to Jeremiah (Jer. 26:14): the fidelity of those covenanted to God in love respond to the call of God with a *"Here am I."* Mary appropriates and perfects this willing response in a way that enables the Advent of our Messiah.

Mary also describes herself as "…the servant of the Lord," sometimes translated as the "maidservant" or "handmaid" of the Lord. These are all titles of submission, all titles of surrender. To the undeified mind, they can sound like terms indicating misogyny. Nothing could be further from the truth. For the entire human family is feminine vis-à-vis the eternal and triune God. Our being as creatures is altogether "received." Our proper attitude and disposition to the Lord, therefore, is necessarily receptive, one of surrender. Those who cannot appreciate the docility of Mary, but insist on deconstructing it with psychological or social categories, prove themselves impervious to fructification by God's Holy Spirit. For the Holy Spirit is infinitely sensitive to both the openness and resistance of those He would inseminate with God's Divine Word. As we noted above, Mary received Jesus in her womb because, through supreme openness and trust, she had previously conceived Him in her heart. Either a heart is given over completely in submission to the one it loves, or it remains forever aloof, substituting fruitless speculation as a sad surrogate for impassioned surrender. Mary's heart was anything but aloof. It was given over without reservation to the One she desired to receive.

We glimpse here the true meaning of chastity and virginity. These are the polar opposites of asexuality or disinterested love. They refer instead to a form of impassioned commitment that brooks no rival. "Purity of heart," Kierkegaard said, "is to will one thing." Mary willed one thing: "To love God with her whole heart, mind, and soul, and to love her neighbor as herself" (Lev. 19:18). Only the undivided heart is capable of conception. Only the heart impassioned and on fire with love is able to be fruitful. Chastity and fruitfulness are identical in the heart of the one who truly loves. Neither virginity nor chastity have anything to do with a particular state of life. Or, rather, they apply with equal importance to all states of life. I surrender myself, body and soul, in service and submission to the one I love. I do this appropriately to my state in life. Giving myself fully and unconditionally in physical, emotional, and spiritual submission constitutes virginity and chastity in marriage. Withholding myself in any of these ways constitutes a violation of my vow. Similarly in the single or religious life: I give my body and soul to the Lord alone, reserving for Him whom I serve exclusive privileges over my person. Chastity and virginity are impassioned and complete surrender; never are they prudish or ashamed withholdings.

Thus we see in Mary the mysterious symbiosis of docility and single-mindedness that constitute her status as "servant" of the Lord. She is without agenda or initiative, yet filled with passion and self-possession. In her prayerful and poised willingness to hear His word and respond to His summons, she is the unsullied virgin perfectly prepared to be the mother of the Lord. St. Irenaeus, the earliest Church Father to cast Mary as the New Eve, may also have had the Blessed Mother in mind when he described the posture we must assume if they which to be deified by Christ: "Offer Him a soft and pliable heart and retain the shape which your fashioner gave you. Retain the moisture he gives you, for if you turn hard and dry you will lose the imprint of his fingers. If you retain the shape he gives you, you will advance to perfection. The mud in you will be hidden by the handiwork of God. His had created your substance; it will overlay you, inside and out, with pure gold and silver (cf. Ex. 25:11), and so adorn you that the king himself will desire your beauty (cf. Ps. 45:11)...For creating belongs to the generosity of God; being created belongs to the nature of humankind. If therefore you offer him what is yours, that is, faith in him and subjection, you shall be the recipient of his handiwork and shall become a perfect work of God."[48]

"...let it be with me according to your word..."

Here we encounter Mary's famous *fiat*: God's most humble and anonymous creature giving the Creator permission to achieve in and through her whatever His ineffable Plan may include. It is an incredible and counter-intuitive mystery that the Lord of all creation is in any way dependent upon his creatures to accomplish in them what He has planned from "before the foundation of the world" (Eph. 1:4; cf. Mt. 25:34; Jn. 17:24; Heb. 4:3; Rev. 13:8). And yet, this is exactly what Mary's *fiat* implies. Like St. Thérèse who said that

---

[48] St. Irenaeus, *Against the Heretics* IV.39.2-3, cited in Denis Minns, *Irenaeus: An Introduction,* 77.

Create WITH God...

although God can certainly do anything without us, He rarely does anything without our involvement, Mary gives witness to the almost unbelievable fact that it pleases the Creator to elicit the cooperation of the creature to achieve the greatest of His miracles. St. Augustine said something similar when he insisted that though God *created* us without our consent, He will not *save* us without it. Mary's fiat reveals a truth about her Lord's love and nature that leaves us incredulous. She reveals to us a God who places Himself, in a sense, at our mercy at the very moments when He desires to render us the greatest good.

Our thinking about God is therefore redeemed when we begin to see that our call to God's service – like Mary's identity as "servant of the Lord" – reflects and participates in the Father's own "servitude" within the Trinitarian *Communio*, as well as in His solicitude for the creation He made through and for His Son. In other words, God's own nature within both the immanent and economic Trinity is one of deference and mutual self-dispossession. God "elicits" Mary's consent because His own love – His very nature as Love – not only has nothing "forced" or "imposed" about it, but it is intrinsically and essentially other-directed and service-oriented. *Wow.* There is no resentment in God. As Balthasar says, He only invites, He never compels.[49]

Try to practice this... invite & elicit people. Do not insist or expect with or from them.

Like the Blessed Mother, we most resemble God Himself when we invite and elicit, never when we insist or expect. Among fallen human persons, expectations, whether of God or other human beings, are but premeditated resentments. The Lord calls, Mary responds. He proposes, Mary consents. In the end, the Father renders Himself powerless in Mary's life – and in the economy of Redemption – until His little Nazarene handmaiden gives Him permission to possess her completely through the power of His Holy Spirit. "The whole world is waiting," wrote St. Bernard of Clairvaux, "prostrate at your feet... since upon your word depends the consolation of the wretched, the redemption of the captives, the liberation of the condemned...the

---

[49] Hans Urs von Balthasar, *The Grain of Wheat: Aphorisms*, 80.

salvation of all the sons of Adam, of your whole race."[50] Mary's *fiat*, like our own, is, by God's grace, essential and indispensable to the earthly fulfillment of His providential plans. *or "Yes" to God now.*

The word of God is enough for Mary. She demands no sign or miracle validating or confirming the promise of the Lord. In this she shows herself greater than the saints of the Old Covenant who requested proof of the validity of the Lord's word (e.g., Ex. 4:1ff.; Jdg. 6:36ff.), and a counter-point to the "adulterous and evil generation" that her Son would speak of subsequently "that demands a sign from God. But no sign will be given to it except the sign of Jonah" (Mt. 16:4). Jonah, of course, is a proto-type of Jesus' resurrection. Mary, in a sense, is already living in the Light of His Resurrection, as faith, hope and love rise and coalesce in her heart in response to the word of God.

[margin: Jesus, as God's word should be enough for us as well]

Mary is a woman of the word. Her word is her life. Her Yes is her identity. She gives her word of faith and obedience in a response complete commitment to the word of the Father. In exchange, she receives His Word: now not simply the prophetic word conveyed by the angel, but the Incarnate Word of His Son, conceived in her by the power of the Holy Spirit.

[margin: We give God our word]

His mission now accomplished, the angel Gabriel *"departed from her."* He too is a being of perfect obedience. In the Mystery of the Annunciation, we see the simplicity of both angelic and human holiness. There are no histrionics, no wasted energy. Neither the angel nor the *Immaculata* play games. Gabriel comes, unannounced, bearing a message and an invitation. Mary responds, first with her questions for discernment, then with her considered consent. Saints neither defer nor dally. They come straight to the point once they discern clearly the word and Will of God. They do not delay in taking the decision to which the Lord invites them, once it is evident which

[margin: He gives us his word (Jesus)]

---

[50] St. Bernard of Clairvaux, Supr missus est 4, 8; PL 183, 83D, quoted in Luigi Gambero, *Mary in the Middle Ages: The Blessed Virgin Mary in the Thought of Medieval Latin Theologians*, 134.

path they should take. They are not afraid of commitment. They see the road less traveled as the King's Highway, and they make haste to take it once they know for certain that it is His voice that beckons them. In all of their actions, they neither shirk nor preempt.[51] They move forward with the alacrity that comes from their faith and trust in God. Their confidence is founded on the promises of a Father who unconditionally keeps them.[52] They know that God is faithful, even if they should fall and falter. Even if we deny Him, He cannot deny Himself (2 Tim. 2:13). His fidelity is our salvation. His faithfulness is our righteousness. Being "delivered from the powers of darkness" (Col. 1:13) means being taken up into the "faithfulness of Jesus Christ" (Rom. 1:18-32; 3:9-10; 3:21-22; Gal. 2:16, 20; Phl. 2:8).[53] This means that, sharing in His relationship of trinitarian intimacy with the Father, we obtain, in Him, a participation in His unbreakable bond with the Father and the Holy Spirit, and are assimilated into His saving death and resurrection. Mary receives all of this in anticipation of, and as the ecclesial archetype and mediatrix of, all subsequent believers who will be saved "not by works of the law but by the faithfulness of Jesus Christ" (Gal. 2:16).

---

[51] Thomas Merton, *Seeds of Contemplation*, 65-69.

[52] See Scott Hahn, *A Father Keeps His Promises*.

[53] The ultimate meaning of "salvation" is "participation in the *pistis Christou*, i.e., in 'the faithfulness of Jesus to His Father.'" Adopting a "participative" approach to our Life "in Christ," as well as contemplating the "faithfulness of Christ" vis-a-vis His Father are key to understanding salvation as *theosis*, i.e., as deification, becoming 'partakers of the divine nature' (2 Pt. 1:4). For an extended discussion of both the "participative perspective" and the "faithfulness of Christ" (*pistis Christou*) as developed by St. Paul, see Wright, *Pauline Perspectives: Essays on Paul*, 529-533.

Visitation

$\mathcal{L}$uke 1:39-40

"In those days Mary set out and went with haste to a Judean town in the hill country, where she entered the house of Zechariah and greeted Elizabeth"

Mary's being responds to the *gravitas* of the moment. She knows something infinitely dramatic underway. She is dimly aware of her seminal role in what is transpiring, but she is oblivious to the infinite implications shimmering down from her *fiat*. She moves forward *in haste*, leaving in her wake uncountable numbers of waves, rippling and rolling across the ocean of history, until all that God is accomplishing through her washes up peacefully upon the shores of eternity (cf. Rev. 12:17).

She knows that Elizabeth is also involved. The angel has told her as much. Yet, it is neither information nor insight that compels Mary forward. It is her deeper, inarticulate intuition. It is her divinely-inspired sense that she and her cousin and everyone before and after them is involved in an orchestrated miracle of the God of Abraham, Isaac, and Jacob that far exceeds and infinitely transcends what the human actors can conceptualize or conceive of. She goes in haste, therefore, "she-knows-not-why," but with a most compelling sense of "go-she-must."

No doubt Mary's trip was arduous. It is journey she would make again eight months later in response to the summons to be registered, with Joseph, in the town of their forefathers. Did she have any premonition that this is way her Son would also journey on his way "up to Jerusalem" to enters into His Passion? "Mary did you know?"[54] Was the Mother aware that she was already preceding her Son to the place of His suffering and our salvation? How deeply was the sword promised by Simeon in the Temple already penetrating Mary's heart? Did she have any sense of the hill country of Judea prefiguring the Hill of Calvary upon which Her Son would give His life for the life of the world? Probably not. As always, Mary's concern was not for herself but for the ones she was seeking to serve. She is solicitous for Elizabeth, not for herself. Thus, she travels in haste, traversing many, many miles up-and-down, hither-and-yon, finally making the last and most difficult climb to reach the house of Zechariah and Elizabeth.

Did Mary arrive at Ein Kerem totally exhausted? No matter. Her expenditure of love causes her – as with every great saint – not to count the cost. She is happy to extend herself for the sake of the beloved. She thinks only of Elizabeth and her needs, nothing of her own tired and dusty condition.

"...and she entered the house of Zechariah and greeted Elizabeth..."

Zechariah is the head of this household, Elizabeth is the heart. Now comes the virgin mother (Mary) to embrace the formerly sterile couple. A marriage is no less a marriage just because children have not been given it. Nuptial unity, covenantal, marital commitment mirror the triune God whether or not offspring proceed from a fruitful womb. Still, the conception of Zechariah and Elizabeth is a holy miracle, reminding us once again of Abraham and Sarah (Gen. 18:1-15). "She who was thought barren – (and forsaken of God) – "has been found fruitful" (Lk. 1:36; cf. 23:29). Both Mary and Elizabeth reveal that barrenness betokens – in the lives of those who

---

[54] The title of the now famous Christmas song, with lyrics written by Mark Lowry and music written by Buddy Greene. For a beautiful recording of this song search: http://www.bing.com/videos/search?q=mary+did+you+know&view=-detail&mid=6DDF4ED3B95FB7B365286DDF4ED3B95FB7B36528&-FORM=VIRE.

love God – a purity of heart and an internal virginity from which the Lord is often pleased to cause salvific fruit to grow.

Barren ground becomes fertile ground when nothing exists in it save a deep-down receptivity to the seed planted there; receptivity, that is, to the One alone who can satisfy what the ground seeks by nature. Solitude is not loneliness when its innermost center is focused in faith, hope, and love on the God of Abraham, Isaac, and Jacob. Elizabeth, therefore, continues the tradition of Sarah. She who was thought to be worthless in the sight of God is made by Him into a paradoxical and attention-getting instrument of His divine promises and His inscrutable providential mercy (Gen. 11:30; cf. 25:21; 29:31).

Mary rejoices in Elizabeth's conception. Not only because of what God will do through her by giving birth to John the Baptizer, Mary's Son's Forerunner, but also because of the gift Elizabeth is in her own right: a person, like Mary herself, open and surrendered to the 'God of the impossible,' one available to His purposes, even in her advanced age. Mary admires and even seeks, in a sense, to imitate her older cousin, despite knowing intuitively that in the divine economy she (Mary) has no equal.

"Mary greeted Elizabeth..." Does she acknowledge Zechariah? Doubtless she does. Yet, Zechariah's "house" provides but the strong framework wherein the fertile ground of Elizabeth, and the Enclosed Garden who is Mary, may come together and share the unutterable Wisdom that they have been made fruitful with from on high. Nothing external or pedestrian is intended here. Luke is pointing to the deep, dark, feminine openness that – as symbolic of the attitude humanity should always have vis-à-vis Father, Son, and Holy Spirit – makes the redemption of the world and the re-creation of human nature possible. The Incarnation has already occurred. It's effects are just beginning to manifest (cf. Rev. 21:5)

"When Elizabeth heard Mary's greeting, the child leapt in her womb. And Elizabeth was filled with the Holy Spirit"

St. Paul tells us, "Faith comes through hearing" (Rom. 10:17). St. John tells us, "In the beginning was the Word" (Jn. 1:1). Genesis tells us, "And God said, 'Let there be light,' and there was light" (Gen. 1:3). The power of God's Word, from beginning to end in the Bible, is creative. It is all-powerful. It creates entire worlds, both visible and invisible. It is "before all else that is" (Col. 1:17).

In this verse, the words of Mary enter the ears of Elizabeth. The Word in Mary's womb reaches out, through His mother's words, to enter the ears and womb of Elizabeth. There He touches and recreates the one (John the Baptizer) who himself later will exclaim, "I am the friend of the bridegroom, who stands and hears him, who rejoices greatly at the bridegroom's voice. For this reason my joy has been fulfilled" (cf. Jn. 3:29). John is filled with joy at the coming of Christ – the Divine Bridegroom - into his world. The Redeemer is already exercising His mission and identity as the re-creative and salvific Word of the Father, and John is already heralding Jesus' identity in the womb of Elizabeth. John is also the first one "made clean" by the touch of Jesus, responding with joy to the advent of the Incarnate Word in the womb of Mary. Mary conveys the Savior to His Forerunner and he is immediately reborn in Jesus. John is "consecrated in truth" (Jn. 17:19) through the mediation of the Redeemer and His Mother.

"Leaping with joy" at the appearance of the Redeemer is neither peculiar nor confined to the Savior's Forerunner. Using Matthew as an example, we can conjecture that when Jesus called each of His apostles, they "leapt" from where they were and what they were doing and followed Him (Mt. 4:20; 9:9). And how many other instances in the public ministry of the Lord do we not see the lame and the crippled, the downcast and downtrodden "leap with" joy and new hope at the coming of the Christ (e.g., Mk. 10:50). When Jesus is passing by, those in need of new life leap from where they are and come harkening unto Him. Neither hell nor high water can keep those in need of a Savior from leaping from where they are to be where He is (cf. Jn. 14:3).

Here we see Jesus as the Fount and Fulfillment of those who "leapt for joy" in the history leading up to His appearance in the flesh. We recall David "leaping" unashamedly in joy before the Ark of the Covenant, giving the lie to the sardonic skepticism of his wife, Michal (2 Sam. 6:16), as well as intimating the reverence appropriate to Jesus as the Bread of Life and the Word of God,[55] and the respect due His Mother, the New, more perfect, Ark of the Covenant. The prophet Malachi also promises that "for you who revere my name the sun of righteousness shall rise, with healing in its wings. You shall go out leaping like calves from the stall" (Mal. 4:2). David, John the Baptist, Jesus' apostles, and all those He cured surely fulfill this prophecy. But it is the Sun of Righteousness Himself – Jesus – who precedes and exceeds in "leaping" and "joy" those who respond to His Arrival in this manner. In the Song of Songs we read: "The voice of my beloved! Look, he comes, leaping upon the mountains, bounding over the hills. My beloved is like a gazelle or a young stag. Look, there he stands behind our wall, gazing in at the windows, looking through the lattice. My beloved speaks and says to me: 'Arise, my love, my fair one, and come away; for now the winter is past, the rain is over and gone" (Sg. 2:8-11). Jesus' love surpasses our own. Our passion for Him is infinitely exceeded by His Passion for us.

[55] Showbread and copies of the Torah were kept in the Ark of the Covenant. See Heb. 9:4.

Indeed, it is more accurate to say that our joy for Jesus is a function, consequence, and dim intimation of the passion and joy with which the Eternal Word "leapt down" to us in love in order to gather the fallen human family back into the Trinitarian Embrace.

Ultimately it is to the Trinity itself that we must ascend to discover the real source of all leaping and joy. The passion with which David dances for joy before the Ark, the excitement with which John the Baptist leaps for joy at the words of Mary, and the gratitude of those cured by the Savior who leap for joy upon their deliverance: all of these are but an images of the passion, love, and joy with which the Persons of the Trinity "leap" in love eternally towards each other and towards us. They go out of themselves for themselves in ways unimaginable to our finite minds. Yet, the deep-down joy we experience in being loved by another – especially when that Other is Jesus – is a true, if limited, image and echo of what transpires among Father, Son, and Holy Spirit. When John leaps for joy in his mother's womb, he is responding as the Savior would have all of us do to the coming of Christ. Still, it is crucial to remember that "… it is not you who have chosen Me, I have chosen You (Jn. 15:16)… it is not that we have loved God, but that He has loved us first" (1 Jn. 4:19). The joy and leaping passion within the Trinity transcends all human experience of love or joy, while at the same time is the primordial reality that makes them possible and meaningful.

"…and Elizabeth was filled with the Holy Spirit…"

The Holy Spirit takes possession of Elizabeth. She is overcome by the Spirit. An experience more powerful than the descent of the *Shekinah* (Ex. 40:38; Nm. 9:15; 1 Kg. 8:10-11) has occurred within her. The babe within her womb (John) has become by grace what the babe in Mary's womb (Jesus) is by nature: God. "God became man," said St. Athanasius, echoing the entire patristic tradition, "so that human being could become God."[56] This is no exaggeration. John the Baptist is the first sinful human person who is divinized by the power of the Holy Spirit working in tandem with the Incarnation. John's deification occurs when the Holy Spirit fills the person of Elizabeth. He is given a share in the Son's Salvation – i.e., His relationship with His Father – through the direct intervention of the Holy Spirit. John is totally sanctified. He is freed from original sin and established in holiness, set apart, as it were, even as an infant, for the mission he would assume as Forerunner of the Redeemer. Like Mary, he is freed from Original Sin and from all actual sin because of his role as the primary herald of the Lamb of God (Jn. 1:29, 36).

Despite their special status, however, Elizabeth is not Mary and John is not Jesus. What the Holy Spirit is doing in and for John and his mother (Elizabeth) is not of the same order as the relationship enjoyed by Mary and Jesus with the Holy Spirit. Mary is the sinless mother of the sinless Redeemer. Elizabeth is the sinful mother of the sanctified Forerunner. At this precise moment in Mary's visitation of Elizabeth, Jesus, Mary, and John are all without sin, but for importantly different reasons and in fundamentally different ways. Jesus is God by nature and therefore totally without sin. Mary is sinless by way of preservation – a trinitarian intervention "before the foundation of the world" - in light of the merits of Her Son's redemptive death and resurrection.[57] John is divinized by the Holy Spirit in a way that mirrors the sinlessness of Jesus and Mary but in no way equals it.

We see cascading here the incorporative and overflowing Trinitarian Life, communicated by the Father in the Incarnate Son through the Holy Spirit. The Eternal Word (Jesus) is made man in the womb of the immaculate virgin Mary in order to impart a participative share in His divine nature to those human persons who are

---

[56] St. Athanasius, *On the Incarnation*, 54.

[57] It is this conviction of the Church that led to the proclamation of the dogma of the Immaculate Conception.

But we can only be receptive by Grace, right?

receptive to His Holy Spirit. Jesus is a Divine Person who assumes a human nature in the womb of Mary. As God, He becomes man without ceasing to be a Divine Person. John the Baptist is the first sinful human person who assumes a divine nature in the womb of Elizabeth. As a man, he becomes God without ceasing to be a human person.[58] This is the incredible doctrine of deification *(theosis)* that so characterized the deepest theological reflection on the mystery and purpose of the Incarnation in the early church.[59] Blessed are they who are not scandalized by the enormity of its impact or the mystical dimensions of its paradoxical expressions.

Deification – rightly understood – leads to consummate humility. Mary is exalted because she was humble. Yet, the more she is exalted ('...all generations will call me blessed'), the more unassuming she becomes. So too with John the Baptist who, through grace obtained from Christ, receives his *immaculate re-conception* in the womb of his mother, Elizabeth. He leaps for joy in response to the divinizing presence of his Redeemer; yet, his "leaping" is simultaneously a "bowing down," a kenosis (self-surrender). It is an acknowledgement (in typological fulfillment of Jacob and Esau stirring in the womb of their mother, Rebekah [Gen. 25:22-23]) that, as John would say later, "He must become greater, I must become lesser" (Jn. 3:30). John indicates in his first intentional movement as a babe in his mother's womb what his role and mission, identity and initiative would be throughout his life and ministry: a herald and friend of the Bridegroom, not His rival or equal. John knows

---

[58] The mystery of the Great Exchange that took place in the Incarnation is even more profound than this sentence states. As St. Maximus the Confessor puts it: 'A firm pledge of hope for deification is given to human nature by the Incarnation of God, which makes man divine in the same measure as that in which God was made human" (*Cap. theol. dogm. cent.* I, c.62; PG, XC, 1204).

[59] For an exhaustive study of the early church's doctrine of deification, see Norman Russell's magisterial study, *The Doctrine of Deification in the Greek Patristic Tradition*. See also *Partakers of the Divine Nature: The History and Development of Deification in the Christian Traditions*, ed., Michael J. Christensen and Jeffery A. Wittung.

himself to be not the Master but the servant, not the Hero but the hero's best friend. John's expression of joy is not for what Christ has done for him (brought salvation, deification) but for Who Jesus is in Himself. John responds to Jesus not because of the work He has accomplished but because of the Divine Word, the Divine Person, Who He is. John is content to be the one whose sole happiness is to serve, protect, proclaim, defend, and, if necessary, to die witnessing to the One who alone is "worthy" to receive glory and honor and power, wealth and wisdom and might, honor and glory and blessing!' (Rev. 4:12; 5:12). With John, as with Mary, we see that their deification results in *kenosis*: deliverance from obsession with self issuing in joyful self-surrender and unconditional service to the Master. For did not Jesus Himself say, "I have come to serve, not to be served" (Mt. 20:28), and "as I have done, you must likewise do" (Jn. 13:15).

"She exclaimed with a loud cry, 'Blessed are you among women, and blessed is the fruit of your womb...'"

Elizabeth "cried out with a loud voice..." She cries out, in a sense, like a woman in labor. It is as if she is giving birth to something within herself even greater than John the Baptist. She is giving prophetic utterance to something that wells up in her, the content and impact of which exceeds her human understanding. In so doing she also fulfills the prophecy Mary uttered a few weeks earlier: "...all generations shall call me blessed" (Lk. 1:48). Elizabeth is the first of twenty centuries of true believers who "worship" Mary. That is, Elizabeth sets the pattern for those, inspired by the Holy Spirit, who, in confessing Mary to be the Mother of God (*Theotokos*), grant her, not the adoration (*latrea*) due the Trinity alone, but the unique veneration (*hyper-dulia*) accorded no other human person. Fervent devotion to Mary of the sort Elizabeth gives here – the spontaneous, 'loud,' uncontainable acclamation of the Mother's key presence in the dramatic deliverance her Jesus brings to the world - remains the single most defining litmus test for true devotion to Jesus. In other words, true devotion to Mary is the shortest and surest way to orthodox adherence to Christ.[60] The mystery of Mary's indispensable role and singular status before the Father remains a scandal to those who reject such a pre-eminent role for Mary in the drama

---

[60] See St. Louis de Montfort's spiritual classic, *True Devotion to Mary*. Recall also that the it was at the Council of Ephesus in 351 a.d., that Mary was acclaimed *Theotokos*, God-bearer, Mother of God. This, in contradistinction to the heretical view of Nestorius, who called Mary only "Mother of Christ."

of Redemption. Yet, as John Henry Cardinal Newman often said - himself a convert from Protestantism - wherever deep devotion to Mary is missing, equally deep denial of Christ's divinity is not long in following. In a manner, therefore, paralleling and sharing in the inseparability of the Persons within the Trinity, Mother and Son *belong together* in the work of Jesus Christ. It is because Jesus is inseparable from Mary in the divine economy that Mary merits the *hyper-dulia* (extreme devotion/honor) we accord her, and which calls forth such an acclamation of praise we hear here in the words of Elizabeth. Any Christology that minimizes or outright denies the eternally-decreed and incarnationally-evident union of Mother and Son in the drama of salvation obscures the Mystery of Christ and takes away from the fullness of Revelation.

The little word "and" guarantees Mary's singularity – and legitimates our undying devotion to her – in the drama of salvation. She is "blessed among women" *and* "blessed [because of] the fruit of her womb." It is almost inconceivable to those who do not fully appreciate the bond of Father and Son within the Trinity, and the bonding [and separating] power of their Holy Spirit, that in Mary we can discern how God "has need of us" in a way that both parallels and participates in His triune communion. Mary is "blessed among women" because she carries Jesus in her womb. He is the Light of the World and the Savior of humankind. But for all of that, Mary's unique identity as a woman – daughter, mother, spouse – is not unimportant. Though her mission defines her identity in and for Jesus, this very identity purifies, perfects, and vivifies what is uniquely charming and endearing in her personality as Miriam of Nazareth. Devotion to Mary as Mother of the Redeemer is not in competition with, nor does it in any way lessen, our love of her as a special person in her own right. Like each of us, she is created as an unrepeatable, incommunicable, and utterly unsubstitutable person. She is made thus by God, yes, in light of her mission, but also like us, first and foremost for the Lord's sheer delight of expressing and pouring His love into creatures He has made in His own image and likeness. Personal uniqueness is increased and enhanced, not eliminated or diminished, as we enter more deeply into the mission God has given us. Every saint is exquisitely unique. This is a mystery of God's non-competitive co-inherence with the Mystical Body of Christ that He has created to communicate His love to the world. It is also a mystery affirmed in our devotion to Mary as uniquely special person, a devotion that is the necessary and legitimate complement to our adoration of her Son.

Mary is also "blessed among women" because she recalls and brings to perfection the long history of heroic Israelite women chosen by God to further His purposes. "Through the prophets, God forms his people in the hope of salvation, in the expectation of a new and everlasting Covenant...such holy women as Sarah, Rebecca, Rachel, Miriam, Deborah, Hannah, Judith, and Esther kept alive the hope of Israel's salvation. The purest figure among them is Mary."[61] In this passage, Elizabeth blesses Mary with the same words spoken to Jael and Judith in the Old Covenant (Jdg. 5:24-27; Jud. 13:18). Jael and Judith were praised because of their heroic faith and courage in leading the defeat of enemies hostile to God's chosen people. Each of them eliminated enemy commanders by dealing them mortal blows to the head. This Mary will also do, but on a scale and in a manner at once transcending and vindicating these holy women who preceded her. Mary it is who, in concert with her Son, "crushes the head of the serpent" (cf. Gen. 3:15), "the ancient enemy" (Rev. 12:9; 20:2), "the liar and father of lies, a murderer from the beginning" (Jn. 8:44). Mary stands at the end of the drama of redemption as the "woman clothed with the sun," on her head a "crown of twelve stars" (Rev. 12:1). [A]fter a long period of waiting the times are fulfilled in her, the exalted Daughter of Sion, and the new plan of salvation is established."[62]

---

[61] CCC #64
[62] LG 55, cited in *CCC* #489.

"And blessed is she who believed that there would be a ful-
fillment of what was spoken to her from the Lord"

"Blessedness" is accredited to Mary because she is a woman of faith. This title is *attributed* to her, not "imputed" to her, as in the forensic theology of Luther or Calvin. Mary receives the same joyous acknowledgement as one of God's "righteous" or "just" ones – just like Abraham (cf. Rom. 4:12) (though greater) – because of her faith. "Because" here means "in light of." Not only is Mary's 'righteousness' not the 'imputed righteousness of the Reformation, it is a not covert form of works righteousness either. "Blessed" is the title Mary merits by harkening in obedience to what the angel prophesies. Mary's is a posture of faith in which trust and obedience are identical. Recall that 'Abraham believed God, and it was reckoned to him as righteousness ' (Rom. 4:3). He is the prototype of "justifying faith" because of the concrete obedience he shows responding immediately to the command of God (Gen. 12:1-9). Mary is, in a sense, more deliberate than Abraham (and for this reason more self-possessed and meritorious) in her obedient response to the invitation of God. Yet, both she and Abraham give the lie to the artificial cleavage, common-place since the Reformation, between faith and action, trust and obedience. Such dichotomy is foreign to the Hebrew psyche. *To trust God is to act in obedience to His loving address.* To obey is to be filled with faith. To be filled with faith is to "be zealous with zeal" for the commandments of God (cf. 1 Kg. 19:10, 14). Abraham, Mary, and the entire prophetic tradition of Israel, up to and including St. Paul, the great Apostle of faith, all testify to the fact that spontaneous and joyful obedience to the living Word of God defines the content of biblical faith. Faith working in love is the only kind of faith Scripture acknowledges as "saving" (Gal. 5:6).

There is also a clear and distinct "object" of Mary's faith. She believes *"that there would be a fulfillment of what was spoken to her..."* Her faith attaches itself to an eschatological object. It has a thrust, a term, a *raison-de-etre*. Her faith is of a piece with her hope that *what* the angel has told her would *in fact* come about. This reminds us, not only of the Hebrew mentality for which reality is concrete and God's "mighty deeds" (e.g., Ps. 71:16; Sir. 18:4) occur in history, but of the more sacramental vision of the Letter to the Hebrews which defines faith as "the assurance of things hoped for, the conviction of things not seen" (Heb. 11:1). Faith, if it be truly Christian, truly biblical, always has an object. It is a personal act of trust in a reality or realities independent of human wishing and willing. It is never a non-intentional. Its aim is never amorphous. It always intends definite and distinct objects, albeit objects that are supernatural and mysterious in nature and not given in clear and distinct form to the created human mind.

Ultimately faith is an act of trust in the God who promises a distinct and definite outcome. It is an act of surrender to the One whose trustworthiness we are willing to sake our lives upon. He promises an outcome that both fulfills and transcends history. "We see now as in a mirror darkly," says St. Paul (1 Cor. 13:12), knowing only in part...but when the complete comes, the partial will come to an end' (1Cor. 13:9-10). We mustn't confuse the indistinct outline of His eschatological promises with wish-fulfillment (Freud) or self-projection (Feuerbach). Like Abraham and Mary, if we have faith, we '...are being transformed... from one degree of glory to another' (2 Cor. 3:18). This transformation "illumines" our understanding, but without removing the opaqueness that veils the objects of our faith until such time as the Son of Man "unveils" (*apokalyptsis*) "what he has in store for those that love Him" (1 Cor.

2:9). It is because Mary *believes* that she "sees" that "there will be a fulfillment of what was spoken to her from the Lord." Belief in the heart enables understanding in the spirit. Love in the spirit makes vision in the soul possible. In her heart and in her spirit, Mary "sees" that what the Lord is "revealing" to her will definitely come to pass. She knows Him to be trustworthy. She "knows" and "sees" what He promises to be certain of fulfillment in ways that surpass her ability to comprehend or express. But for all that, they are neither irrational nor inexplicable. The Holy Spirit reveals the truth of God's salvation to Mary at a level "too keep for words" (Rom. 8:26). As spouse of the Holy Spirit, Mary "knows" without being able to express what is revealed to her by the Holy Spirit, just as the Holy Spirit Himself " searches [and knows] everything, even the depths of God" (1Cor. 2:10). She acts on His promises because she knows both the Subject and object of His words to be certain and therefore worthy of her trust.

*"And Mary said, 'My soul magnifies the Lord, and
my spirit rejoices in God my Savior...'"*

We notice immediately two dimensions of Mary's response to
Elizabeth's greeting. Both her "soul" and her "spirit" respond. We
need not tarry with ancient or medieval distinctions between soul
(*psyche*) and spirit (*pneuma*) in order to appreciate an important point
the text reveals to us. In Mary's "soul" magnifying the Lord we see
the natural élan of gratitude that should be demonstrated by all created beings towards their Creator. In the early church, St. Gregory
of Nyssa drew a sharp distinction between creation and the Creator,
between contingent being and Uncreated Being (God).[63] All contingent being – from rocks and stars to amoeba and people – owe
every ounce of their existence to the Creator who in no manner can
be identified with or dependent upon the creatures He has created.
Created reality "participates" in God, in the sense of "drawing and
receiving its very being" from Him. God, however, is not contingent
upon the creation He has made. He sustains it in being; it contributes
nothing to His existence as God. These distinctions are affirmed
and maintained by our belief in creation *ex nihilo* (out of nothing),
but they are easily lost among creatures who, because of Original Sin,
incline towards their own interests in selfish and self-centered ways.
We do not incline naturally, as did Mary, towards our Maker with
hearts and souls filled with wonder and thankfulness. Thus, there

---

[63] See Hans Boersma, *Embodiment and Virtue in Gregory of Nyssa: An Anagogical
Approach*, 51.

is a kind of "natural union" with God[64] enjoyed by all creatures by virtue of their very creation that Mary acknowledges and praises by "magnifying the Lord" with her "soul." It is an intrinsic sort of gratitude that also characterized our first parents, Adam and Eve, prior to their fall from grace by sin. Saints are those who, by following Mary's example and imitating her attitude of gratitude, re-acquire a natural joy for God in their souls, enabling them connaturally, as it were, to magnify the Lord in even the simplest of their actions.[65]

We see in Mary another, more intentional response. For she says, "my spirit rejoices in God my Savior." Leaving aside for the moment the focal point of Mary's praise – "God my Savior" – we can allow ourselves to be arrested by the freedom with which Mary begins her hymn of joy. In addition to the spontaneous, almost instinctual response of her "soul," Mary's "spirit" also rejoices, but

---

[64] St. John of the Cross distinguishes between our 'substantial,' 'common' or 'sustaining union' with God, and a 'participative' or 'transformative' union with God - the 'union of likeness,' as he says - which is our divinization in Christ. "God sustains every soul...even though it may be that of the greatest sinner in the world...[this union] always exists, but the soul's union with and transformation in God does not always exist, except when there is likeness of love...[then] God and the soul become one in participant transformation, and the soul appears to be God more than a soul. Indeed, it is God by participation." *Ascent to Mt. Carmel*, II.5.3. See also: *Spiritual Canticle*, XXVI.5-11; *Living Flame of Love*, I,3-4, 16; IV.14-16.

[65] See above, n. 65. See also, Andrew Tallon's description of the connatural virtues that obtain in the life of deified persons in *Head and Heart: Affection, Cognition, Volition as Triune Consciousness*, 222ff. Thomas Merton espouses the same view when he notes: "A saint is capable of loving created things and enjoying the use of them and dealing with them in a perfectly simple, natural manner, making no formal references to God, drawing no attention to his piety, and acting without any artificial rigidity at all...without any explicit reference to God, in such a way that his statement gives greater glory to God and arouses a greater love of God than the observations of someone less holy, who has to strain himself to make an arbitrary connection between creatures and God through the medium of hackneyed analogies and metaphors that are so feeble that they make you think there is something the matter with religion...the saint preaches sermons by the way he walks and the way he stands and the way he sits down and the way he picks things up and holds them in his hand..." *New Seeds of Contemplation*, 24, 193.

with a dimension of adulation and adoration that goes beyond and completes her natural élan of praise. She "rejoices in God my Savior" with an interior freedom and self-possessed spirit that reveals to us both the more transformative union we are called to by God.[66] Mary's confident rejoicing in the Lord is essence of true humility. For we can see immediately that humility, as exemplified by Mary's response, does not mean having no self. That is, humility does not involve the elimination of a person's uniquely defining "spirit" (read: personality, identity), or the evisceration of the unrepeatable and incommunicable characteristics that make a person who she or he is. Christianity is not Quietism or Buddhism. It is worlds apart from Oriental or New Age mysticism, the purpose of which is the elimination of the self or the re-absorption of self into a pre-existing, totalitarian Whole. No. The Father of Jesus makes every single person in His image and likeness: equal in dignity but different from every other creature in every other way. Mary is no exception. She is distinctly and uniquely "who she is" in her "spirit." It is in this "spirit" – in this ineluctable and unsubstitutable identity of her very own (and no one else's) - that Mary "rejoices in God my Savior."

We cannot understand the significance of Mary adoring and adulating focus on "God my Savior" without simultaneously appreciating the extent to which Mary, in her supreme self-possession, was her own person, "fully alive" to the graces she experienced God bestowing upon her.[67] Mary's utterance here is fully free of external compulsion. It arises without coercion from the depths of her heart. Hers is an altogether unrestricted and uncompelled assent of joy, a deliberate expression of a person fully in touch with herself, responding freely and responsibly to the One she recognizes as her

---

[66] Cf. n. 64 above…

[67] Here we recall St. Irenaeus' famous saying: "*The glory of God is man fully alive*, and the life of man is the vision of God. If the revelation of God through creation already brings life to all living beings on the earth, how much more will the manifestation of the Father by the Word bring life to those who see God." *Against Heresies*, IV, 20, 7 (emphasis added).

Highest Good (*Summa Bonum*), the fulfillment of her heart's (spirit's) desire.

Self-possession, of course, does not occur in a vacuum. It comes about in relationship, in dialogue. First in our earliest relationships, especially that of an infant and her mother, then through other relationships in our lives, and finally, and quintessentially, in our relationship with God.[68] Human maturity, whether at the natural or supernatural level, is forever a work in progress. Human person-hood is always at once a gift and a task. Mary's natural and super-natural kinds of union with God and her responses to God's gifts testify to this fact. And now she reveals to us that only when we know and appreciate God as "our Savior" do we enter into our full identity as persons, only then do our other relationships acquire the

---

[68] Hans Urs von Balthasar famously uses the image of 'the mother's smile' as the foundational human analogue for the 'real distinction' between Creator and creation and as an anthro-theological image of how both divine and human persons subsist in their relations. Says Balthasar, "The little child awakens to self-consciousness through being addressed by the love of his mother...The interpretation of the moth-er's smiling and of her whole gift of self is the answer, awakened by her, of love to love, when the 'I' is addressed by the 'Thou'; and precisely because it is understood in the very origin that the 'Thou' of the mother is not the 'I' of the child, but both centers move in the same ellipse of love, and because it is understood likewise in the very origin that this love is the highest good and is absolutely sufficient and that, a priori, nothing higher can be awaited beyond this, so that the fullness of reality is in principle enclosed in this 'I'-'Thou' (as in paradise) and that everything that may be experienced later as disappointment, deficiency and yearning longing is only descended from this: for this reason, everything—'I and Thou' and the world—is lit up from this lightning flash of the origin with a ray so brilliant and whole that it also includes a disclosure of God. In the beginning was the word with which a loving 'Thou' summons forth the 'I': in the act of hearing lies directly, antecedent to all reflection, the fact that one has been given the gift of the reply; the little child does not "consider" whether it will reply with love or non-love to its mother's inviting smile, for just as the sun entices forth green growth, so does love awaken love; it is in the movement toward the 'Thou' that the 'I' becomes aware of itself. By giving itself, it experiences: *I give myself.* By crossing over from itself into what is other than itself, into the open world that offers it space, it experiences its freedom, its knowledge, its being as spirit." (*Explorations in Theology, Creator Spirit*, III, 15-16.)

mutual respect and potential for fulfillment ordained by God "in the beginning."[69]

The object of Mary's faith is "God my savior." She knows her absolute dependence on Him. Mary knows that "to be" is to "be delivered from nothingness" by God her savior. She experiences creation and salvation as dimensions of the identical mystery. She knows that all be-ing, all initiative, come from God. Even her poverty is His gift to her. In no way has she anything to offer to Him, even herself. She experiences her ex-istence as one of total dis-self-possession. This activates in her a complete disponibility towards God that can only be called immaculate.[70] True, she makes a gift of herself to God with

---

[69] For a powerful description of the Original Unity experienced by human persons "in the beginning," see John Paul II's exegesis of these phrases in *Man and Woman He Created Them: A Theology of the Body*, 178-179: "If the account of the creation of man in the two versions, that of Genesis 1 and the Yahwist version in Genesis 2, allows us to establish the original meaning of solitude, unity, and nakedness, by this very fact it allows us also to reach the basis of an adequate anthropology, which seeks to understand and interpret man in what is essentially human. The biblical texts contain the essential elements of such an anthropology, which become clear in the theological context of the "image of God." This concept contains in a hidden way the very root of the truth about man revealed by the "beginning," to which Christ appeals in the dialogue with the Pharisees (see Mt 19:3–9) when he speaks about the creation of man as male and female. One must remember that all the analyses we are carrying out here are connected, at least indirectly, with precisely these words. Man, whom God created "male and female," bears the divine image impressed in the body "from the beginning"; man and woman constitute, so to speak, two diverse ways of "being a body" that are proper to human nature in the unity of this image.

[70] 'Disponibility' is a favorite term used by both Hans Urs von Balthasar and his spiritual colleague, Adrienne von Speyr, to describe the attitude of docility, obedience, receptivity, and openness to truth, love, goodness and beauty, both of God and of the world. For them, 'disponibility' means "that the subject lays aside, as it were, its entire subjectivity, so that henceforth it may be nothing but pure openness to understand the object. This renunciation of the subject's personal viewpoint for the sake of better apprehending the reality of the other entails the dismantling of the whole business called prejudice, which stands in the way of a pure apprehension of the object. It requires no small exertion of the subject's spontaneity to bring it to the point of deciding once and for all to be nothing but receptivity. The subject gives up its own word in order to hear only the word of the thing in all its objectivity. It

complete self-possession; yet, more so than us, she knows that even this self-possession is itself a gift from "God my savior." Before St. Paul ever conceived the words, Mary knew in the core of her being that "it is God who is at work in you, enabling you both to will and to work for his good pleasure" (Ph. 2:13).

Mary experiences her "beholdenness" to God at a virginal, inarticulate level unknown to the sinful rest of us. Poverty is not an experience for her; it is a self-evident fact. She knows in every fiber of her existence that she is not her own. All is gift. Therefore, God, for Mary, is not "secondarily" her savior. He is her Deliverer from the beginning. Mary gives the lie to the heresy of deism. God is not first aloof and indifferent, and then, in response to human needing or giving, a Redeemer. He is our Deliverer from all eternity. To be God is to be Creator. To be Creator is to be Deliverer. Israel knew Yahweh first as their Deliverer, then as their Creator. The primary creation for the people of Israel was their deliverance from slavery in Egypt. They were conceived through the seed of Abraham (Gen. 17:5; cf. Jer. 33:26; Rom. 4:13), and coalesced as a community through their passover into the Promised Land.

It should come as no surprise, therefore, that Mary's song of salvation parallels that of Hannah in the Old Testament (1 Sam. 2:1-10). It reflects many other songs of praise in the annals of Israel's history of deliverance (Ps. 89:10, 13; 98:3; 111:9; Sir. 33:12; Hab. 3:18; Mic. 7:7). Yet, the tenor of Mary's Magnificat transcends and sublates all previous intuitions and expressions of Israel's joy at being God's Chosen One. No one gives voice to the gratitude for God's deliverance and His covenant fidelity like the one who knows herself saved

---

is determined not to interrupt things as they try to express themselves. It has made up its mind to do justice to them. This resolution to be just is already an act of love, because it prefers another's good and another's truth to one's own. This attitude of real willingness to listen can never be left behind in the relation of truth. Even when it is reconfigured within another attitude, it is still the immovable basis upon which everything else is built. It must constantly be verified, because it is the index of the rightness and soundness of love." *Theo-Logic, I,* 112-113.

by virtue of her very creation. As the *Immaculata,* Mary's conception and re-creation in Christ coincide. They do so in a way that parallels the eternal in-dwelling of the Father and the Son in the Holy Spirit. The deliverance from sin that we experience as a subsequent gift to our original creation, Mary receives simultaneously in her conception in the mind of God. She is the Immaculate Conception. In a way inconceivable for us Mary is as ecstatically grateful for her creation as she is for her redemption. This keeps her from ever conceiving of her Immaculate Conception as a badge of honor, enabling her to have an appreciation for the giftedness and salvific nature of her creation that we tend to identify only subsequently with our redemption. We see neither God nor His creation in the same pristine sense as shown to Mary by "God her savior." God is never anything other than Savior for her, whereas for us He often appears as a harsh Judge instead of as a merciful Redeemer.

Mary also praises "God my savior" because He has delivered her from her barrenness. God has turned her virginity – thought by many in Israel as a curse (cf. Gen. 11:30; 25:21) – into fruitfulness. She is a desert whom God has transformed into a blooming Garden Enclosed. As Pope Benedict XVI reminds us, this miracle of the Father "begins with Sarah, mother of Issac, who had been barren, but when she was well on in years and had lost the power of giving life, became, by the power of God, the mother of Isaac and so of the chosen people. The process continues with Hannah, the mother of Samuel, who was likewise barren, but eventually gave birth; with the mother of Samson, or again with Elizabeth, the mother of John the Baptizer. The meaning of all these events is the same: salvation comes, not from human beings and their powers, but solely from God – and from an act of his grace."[71]

We see here that only when humanity empties itself of itself can it receive the life-giving Word of God. Fecundity depends on virginal openness. Purity of heart is the pre-condition for divine fruitfulness.

[71] *Co-Workers in the Truth,* 100.

Virginity of spirit – purity of heart – the "I" stripped clean of self-seeking egoism – these alone make it possible for the human "I" to unite with the Divine "Thou." United with God in this way, a divinizing "We" can exist in which we become co-Redeemers with Him who alone has the power to save. We become through participation in Him what He is by nature: God and Redeemer.

When Mary praises "God my savior!" she refers also to her Son whom she has conceived in her womb. "All that the Father has He has given to the Son" (cf. Jn. 8:38, 42; 15:15), and "all that was in Christ has passed over into His Mysteries (i.e., the sacraments of His Church)."[72] This "admirable exchange" begins with Mary. She is the New Ark of the New Covenant. She is the model and mother of the Church. She receives in her person all that the Father would communicate to those He has predestined since "before the foundation of the world" to be "holy and blameless in his sight" (Eph. 1:4; cf. Col. 1:22; 1 Th. 2:10). Mary is, therefore, the bearer and distributer of all graces. She is the Mediatrix in whose heart heaven and earth meet at a holy crossroad. She brings us divine life because she brings us Jesus. "The law was given to us through Moses; grace and truth came through Jesus Christ" (Jn. 1:17). Mary is Mother and disciple of the Savior whom Moses and all the prophets were seeking.

---

[72] Pope St. Leo the Great, *Sermo.* 74.2: PL 54, 298, cited in *CCC*, 1115.

"For he has regarded the low estate of his handmaiden. For behold, henceforth all generations will call me blessed."

For God, to look upon us is for Him to save us. Blessed are they who receive this "divine regard." To be noticed by God is to be loved by Him. "Jesus looked upon the rich young man and loved him" (Mk. 10:21). When the Father looks upon us, as one of the prayers of the Mass remind us, "He sees and loves in us what He sees and loves in Him (Jesus)."[73]

We think of those waiting to be noticed by God in the Bible: Lazarus at the rich man's table (Lk. 16:20 ff.); the blind man sitting at the side of the road, calling out to be seen by Jesus (Mt. 9:27ff.); the lame man sitting helplessly by the Pool of Siloam, waiting for someone to plunge him into the water (Jn. 5:5ff.); Mary of Bethany sitting adoringly at the feet of the Master, his 'obedient disciple," i.e., 'listening learner'(Lk. 10:28-32). Or the saints outside the Bible, such as St. Thérèse of Lisieux, content to be available to the Lord, as unnoticed or unused as a plaything in the corner, happy as she can be simply ing that she has given herself for Him. "As the eyes of servants look to the hand of their master, as the eyes of a maid to the hand of her mistress," the psalmist proclaims, "so our eyes look to the LORD our God, until he has mercy upon us" (Ps. 123:2). This is the beautiful disposition of dis-possession expressed by Mary as she sings of God's merciful gaze upon her lowly estate.

Mary's yearning for God is complemented by her consummate humility. Like all the saints in the Bible she looks expectantly for

---

[73] Prefaces for Sundays in Ordinary Time VII, Roman Rite.

the Messiah of God. Yet, she harbors no illusions of actually "being seen" by Him. She is like the modest guest Her Son describes in the parable: "When you are invited to a banquet, take the most distant seat. Then, if the Master espies you, He may call to you to come up higher" (Lk. 14:12). Mary knows that God calls "each of us by name" (cf. Jn. 10:3), and perhaps she harbors in her heart the desire of every great saint, i.e., that He "wishes to see" me (cf. Mk. 10:49). Yet, it never occurs to her to put herself forward or to consider herself worthy of His specific attention. She is as unselfconscious as she is self-possessed.

God's election of Mary show us that it is those of "low estate" who are most noticed by Him. He abhors the proud but exalts the humble. He "casts the mighty from their thrones but lifts up the lowly" (Lk. 1:52). He even goes so far as to identify Himself with the stranger and the outcast. "Whenever you did to these, the least of my brethren, you did it to me" (Mt. 25:40). Jesus is one with the foreigner, one with the poor. "Remember that you yourselves were once aliens in a strange land" Yahweh tells the Jews (Ex. 22:21). Jesus continues this predilection of His Father in His preference for "tax collectors and sinners" (Mt. 9:10-11). They are His special guests in the seats of honor at the Supper and Wedding Feast of the Lamb (Rev. 19:9). The Church's "preferential option for the poor" is driven by this vision of God "regarding the low estate" of His chosen ones, a divine preference that finds its finest expression in the Father's election of Mary as the Mother of His Son.[74]

In her "lowliness," Mary also embodies and recapitulates the humiliations endured by all of Israel throughout its history (Deut. 26:7; 1 Sm. 9:16; 1Mc. 3:51; 3 Mc. 2:12; 2 Ezra 9:45). It is as if, in Mary, God proclaims, as He did to Samuel, "I have seen the affliction of my people, because their cry has come to me" (1 Sm. 9:16). In Mary

---

[74] We think here, too, of the "little ones" that Mary has appeared to in Church-approved apparitions such as Lourdes and Fatima. It is poor, benighted children, not "the great and mighty," to whom Mary has entrusted messages from heaven.

God effects the reversal of Israel's fortunes as barren and oppressed. Mary's fruitful virginity overturns Israel's fruitless philandering; her exultation at the hand of God her Savior reverses the degradation endured by Israel at the hands of its enemies (e.g. Judg. 20).

As His "handmaiden," Mary possesses nothing of her own. Her identity is one of attentive service. Her very being is "oriented towards the other." In this she parallels, and participates in, Her Son's procession in the Trinity. His too is *pros ton theon* (πρὸς τὸν θεόν), 'turned towards' or 'facing" God. Like her Son, Mary has no thought for herself. Yet, she is neither maudlin nor artificially modest. She indulges neither in self-pity nor self-deprecation. These facsimiles of true humility are the result of sin. There is no sin in Mary. Therefore, she exhibits none of the histrionics or pseudo-piety that have too often characterized her adulators.

In Jesus and Mary, obedience and receptivity come naturally. They show us what human nature was created to be. Neither Mother nor Son is affected by the fear of death. Thus, they do not indulge in either self-aggrandizement or self-denunciation, that result from pride. They engage in no "heroic projects."[75] Instead, they exhibit true courage and humility. They have integrated the gifts of self-possession and self-donation that image forth God. They know what it is to "be in communion" with Another. They are neither defensive nor demanding. On the contrary, they are open to other without being absorbed by them, responsive to their needs without being resentful for the demands made upon them.

Following her Son's obedient, self-donation within the Trinity, Mary is the Father's perfect handmaiden. She discovers and fulfills the "I" God made her to be. She naturally sees herself as the servant of the "Thou" who created and summons her. Mary can find no better descriptive for herself than "handmaiden" because she

---

[75] "Heroic projects" is the term Ernest Becker uses to describe the futile efforts human beings make to deny their inherent contingency, efforts which, in Becker's opinion, account for the evil we see in the world. See his *The Denial of Death*.

experiences of God as "my Savior." His is initiative, hers the obedient response. She sees herself as an instrument of God's purposes. Yet, there is nothing "mechanical" about her relationship with Him, even though she is absolutely "instrumental" to the salvation of the world.[76] This instrumentality is of a supremely personal, relational nature. She serves Him in tender humility. Her motherhood, warmth, and unique personality are all enhanced and enriched in her role as his "lowly handmaiden." She blooms in her modesty before Him, even as He delights in her innocence.

Mary is aware of the gravitas of the moment. "Behold," she exclaims, "henceforth all generations will call me blessed!" (Lk. 1:48). To the untrained ear this may sound like arrogance or pride. But in truth it is consummate humility. Mary is able to look at herself objectively. Humility is truth. In this moment, Mary is given a taste of the foreknowledge granted only to angels. She sees what "all generations" will say in response to God's initiative in her womb. In light of this vision, she allows herself to be showered with the accolades she knows are to come. She sees her own "Fiat" as an opportunity and a catalyst for all generations to give thanks to God for bringing His salvation in its fullness into the world. She now becomes the instrument of God's praise among His people. She becomes the occasion for their more perfect devotion to Him, in addition to herself being the perfect "Reed of God" and "Praise of His glory."[77]

---

[76] St. Irenaeus described Mary as 'the cause of our salvation,' contrasting Mary's obedience with Eve's disobedience. To wit: 'Mary, having a man betrothed [to her], and being nevertheless a virgin, by yielding obedience, become the cause of salvation, both to herself and the whole human race.' *Against Heresies*, III.22.4.

[77] "Reed of God" is the beautiful description of Mary promoted by Caryll Houselander in her book by the same name, and "Praise of Glory" was the name Saint Elizabeth of the Trinity gave herself. It was her firm belief of what Christian vocation is all about.

"For he who is mighty has done great things for me,
and holy is his name."

God's greatness is uniquely linked to Mary's lowliness. He is as Mighty as she is powerless. Yet, both are consumed with divine love. Mary's humility is of a piece with God's holiness. She is his marionette, so to say, whose limpid disposition is inspired and lifted up – exalted and made aflame – with every touch of His Holy Spirit.

In truth, God and Mary cannot be compared. Adoration (*latria*) belongs to God alone. Yet, a certain kind of derivative worship (veneration, *hyper-dulia*) belongs properly to Mary as the special participant in the holiness of God. God is not to be justly compared to any of His creatures or any part of His creation, or even to His creation taken as a whole (pantheism). God is never just "another" because He is "altogether Other" (*totalier altier*). He is, as Gregory of Nyssa puts it, "beyond the beyond."[78] The human tongue is incapable of rendering God adequate praise, much less an accurate description or creaturely comparison. "His greatness cannot be measured," the psalmist reminds us (Ps. 145:3). Yet, for all that, "he who is mighty has done great things for me," Mary says matter-of-factly. His greatness, she shows us, excludes our claims on Him, to be sure, but manifests itself nonetheless in meeting the needs of the lowly and reversing the plight of the poor. God's greatness is

---

[78] St. Gregory of Nyssa says that God is not only "beyond" all that can be thought and desired but "beyond the beyond": *hyper epekeina, In Eccl.*, hom. 7 (PG 44, 732C). Cited by Hans Urs von Balthasar, *Theo-Logic: Theological Logical Theory: The Spirit of the Truth*, III, 238.

greatest in its divine condescension (*kenosis*). He "stoops down," as it were, to abide with the lowliest among His creatures. He is the Lord of the 'little flowers,' just as He is of the high and mighty.[79] In Israel, the Mighty One is the Warrior (Zeph. 3:17) who does "great things" (Dt. 10:21) for His chosen people. He is first and foremost their Deliverer. He rescues His people from slavery (Judg. 6:9). He leads them from Exile to freedom (Ex. 6:7). He comes to the assistance of the downtrodden (Ps. 74:21; 147:6). He makes the barren land fruitful (Ps. 107:37), and He renders the childless fertile (Gen. 25:21; 1 Sam. 1-2). God's greatest greatness seems to consist in His love for the lowly. The fullest extent of His divine transcendence seems to be His desire to be among His people. He is the King of kings who comes among His subjects as one who saves and serves. Mary and God, therefore, are "joined at the hip" (cf. Gen. 32:32) through their respective humilities. Unlike Jacob, however, Mary, in her encounters with God, does not wrestle with Him, but moves is perfect sync with the touches of His Holy Spirit. Thus she receives from Him "great things" that include both wounds (Lk. 2:35) and blessings (Lk. 1:48).

"Holy is his name."

His Name is "Holy," and "Holy" is His "Name." In God, essence and existence are one. Potency and Act are identical. Noun and Adjective are the same. He is what He is. He is Who He Is. "Is" = "Who" = "Father, Son, Holy Spirit" in the Trinity. "In" the Trinity = simply, "Trinity" = "The Three." Who, What, and "He" are synonymous in God.

There is no conceivable way the finite human mind can comprehend the greatness of God. We know Him in His "mighty acts" (Dt. 3:24; Ps. 145:4; cf. Acts. 2:11). "He has shown the might of His arm" (Lk. 1:51). His "strong right arm" has delivered His people

---

[79] St. Thérèse of Lisieux' description of herself as God's 'Little Flower.'

from bondage (Ps. 89:13). He is our liberator and our deliverer (Judg. 3:9, 15). Beyond that, we have little natural knowledge of Him. He makes Himself known in His mighty deeds. Until, that is, He shows Himself in His Son. Jesus is the Human Face of God.[80] He alone knows the Father in Himself. "Himself" here means: In Jesus Himself, and "in the Father" insofar as Jesus "indwells" the Father. The Father, in His innermost identity as Father, remains a Mystery, even to the Son (cf. Jn. 14:28). There is a "distance" between the Father and the Son that the Holy Spirit bridges as their mutual Procession. But the Son is the Father's definitive Word.[81] In His Word, the Father exhaustively expresses and communicates Who He Is. The Life of God is utterly beyond human comprehension. "Eye has not seen, nor ear heard, what God has prepared (in Himself) for those who love Him" (1 Cor. 2:9). Only love, not cognitive speculation, can apprehend God.

Mary exemplifies this love in her prayer. It is in the world of prayer[82] - prayer that flows from love - that the Holy Spirit puts us in contact with the world of God. With Mary as our exemplar and mother in prayer, and with her incomparable intercession, we begin to touch upon something of the mystery of divine holiness. For "holiness" is a participation in the Life of God Himself. Recall that Noun and Adjective are identical in God. God does not "possess" holiness, as if it were a pre-existent quality. His very Divine Personhood is the essence and existence of holiness. Holiness is Who God is. Who and What are synonymous in God. God's Life is

---

[80] See the wonderful book by Christoph Cardinal Schönborn, *God's Human Face: the Christ-Icon*. This is also a favorite theme of Pope Benedict XVI, e.g., "The Face of Christ in Sacred Scripture," in *On the Way to Jesus Christ*, 13-30.

[81] St. John of the Cross tells us that there is no reason to enquire of God in the manner that the prophets did in the Old Testament, nor for him to speak to us or answer us as he did then, because "in giving us, as he did, his Son, who is his one and only Word, he spoke to us once and for all, in this single Word, and he has no occasion to speak further." *Ascent to Mt. Carmel*, II. 22.

[82] See Adrienne von Speyr, *The World of Prayer*.

His goodness, is His love, is His holiness. What we perceive as the "qualities" of God or the "gifts" of God are but refractions of His Trinitarian Mystery. They are given to us in the knowledge of our faith to increase our love for God and to capacitate us to participate more completely in the relationship of Father, Son, and Holy Spirit. "Grace" itself is but a personalist participation in the perichoretic (circular and circulating) love of the Persons of the Trinity. God does not, strictly speaking, "give" grace. He *is* Grace. What He gives is a real share in the relationship He has within Himself as Father, Son, and Holy Spirit. The Holy Spirit is the main Agent of this event, the Son is its singular Instrument, and the Father is its Ultimate Source and Object. The Son brings us to the Father in and through the activity of the Holy Spirit. Holiness consists in entering into the Life of the Trinity. There is nothing mechanical about it. It is altogether a matter of love working through prayer.

According to human etymology, "holy" means "set apart." "Holy things" are things "set apart" – made "sacred" – for the service of God alone. "You shall be a nation 'holy' unto me," God said when He chose the Israelites to be "a light unto the nations" (Ex. 19:6). Both Israel and the "holy" objects and persons of their religion were "set apart" for the purpose of divine worship. They were "chosen from all of the nations" (Jer. 43:5; Tob. 13:5) and priests where "selected from among the people" (Ex. 28:1) for the explicit purpose of glorifying the Name of God and enabling adoration of Him to permeate the entire world (Ex. 9:16; Ps. 8:1). This sharp division between "sacred" things and "secular," between "holy" Israel and the "pagan" nations, finds its origin in God Himself, since He is Holiness itself. Thus, the phenomenon of "holiness," i.e., "setting apart" or "set-apartness" must somehow reflect God's own nature. How so?

Again, Mary is our key. As the only "Holy One," God is utterly different, totally other, altogether separate, indescribably above anything and everything He has created. Holiness as "separateness" stems from, and reveals, the Mystery of God as "totally Other." "'As high as the heavens are above the earth, so high are my ways from yours,' says the Lord. 'My ways are not your ways…'" (Isa. 55:8). With these and many other revelations, God has show us that God and creation cannot be compared. He is 'set apart' from the world. He is the 'Holy' One. Yet, His holiness is not indifference. When Mary proclaims, "God who is mighty has done great things for me, holy is his name," she shows us that the God who is "set apart" from us by nature also "exists for" us as our Creator and Redeemer. She is showing us that though God is "totally other," He is also "totally ours." Or, put more paradoxically: God as Holiness itself is a Self-transcending Mystery of otherness and immanence, alterity and intimacy. He creates us with an independence and autonomy from Himself, yet keeps us united with Himself, even in our sin. And, in His Son, the Father offers us a participation in His own trinitarian Life that not only traverses the distance between us – creature from Creator – but conquers sin and death, making possible our divinization in Him.

We must, therefore, not forget that "holiness" as "setting apart from" yet "existing for" another begins and ends in the Trinity itself. As we have already seen, the Son and the Holy Spirit are "set apart from" the Father in their processions from Him, yet they forever "exist for" Him, and He for them. Holiness is God's very Name (*"Holy is His Name"*). His "nature" is that of a *Communion of Persons* who both "exist for" and are "set apart from" each other. Trinitarian love is the definition of holiness as we experience it. It is Source of all holiness. Or, to put it more properly: human holiness is a participation in the holiness of God. This, in turn, is participation in God Himself who, as a communion of Divine Persons "unmixed yet undivided," "inseparable but unconfused," has created and redeemed us in order to be received by, and into, Him.

"And his mercy is on those who fear him from generation to generation."

Mercy is not primarily a moral term. God's Name is Mercy. He comes to those, like Mary "who fear him." Not with the servile fear or cowering of the indentured slave, but with the reverent awe and respect of the self-surrendering servant. Mary's is a "holy fear." It is the fear of one who knows she is "not God." It is the fear of one who knows she is "set apart from" Him through the infinite distance of creature from Creator, yet as one who "exists for" Him as a "creature beholden." Mary holds herself in immaculate, perpetual readiness (virginity) to be of service to Him and of help to others.

God's mercy is *"on those"* who fear Him. It descends like the dew. It descends like manna from the skies (Ex. 16:31ff.). It "alights upon them" as did His Spirit at Pentecost (Acts 2:1ff.) or like "the dawn from on high" prophesied by Zechariah at the birth of John the Baptizer (Lk. 1:78). God's mercy has something about His holy *Shekinah* about it (Ex. 26:1). What descended with power and majesty, with glory and might, upon the Israelites in the desert now descends upon Mary with delicacy and deliberation at her Annunciation. And it descends with the same lack of fanfare, but with equal power and might, upon *"those who fear him"* as Mary did *"from generation to generation."*

We feel close to Mary across all generations. She is our mother and model in the Faith. The Father's Mercy connects us to her. She leads us to Him by taking us to His Son (Jn. 2:5). His Mercy is reflected in her holy fear as the sun is reflected in the moon. We see in Mary's prayerful disposition what our *disponibility* before the

Trinity should be. But we cannot simply imitate her. She wouldn't want only that. She is our mother but also our fellow disciple. She wishes us to "taste and see the goodness of the Lord" (Ps. 34:8), not merely to admire it from afar. God's Mercy comes to meet us in His *Shekinah* in the Old Covenant (Ex. 25:22; Lev. 16:2; 2 Sam. 6:2; 2 Kin. 19:14, 15; Psa. 80:1; Isa. 37:16; Ezek. 9:3; 10:18; Heb. 9:5), in the Incarnation of Jesus, and in the Holy Spirit who descends upon the first disciples on Pentecost and bedews us ever-afresh in the Mysteries of His Church, as well as the other "natural sacraments of his love" in nature and in our encounters with our neighbor (Mt. 25). Distant from her in years, we are one with Mary in faith. With her we yearn and long for the mercy of God that is *"on those who fear him from generation to generation."*

> *"And Mary remained with Elizabeth about three months and returned to her home."*

Human and divine factors are very much inter-mixed in Mary's visitation with Elizabeth. She "remained with her about three months": the beginning of Mary's pregnancy and the final trimester of Elizabeth's. Hormonally, they help each other. The older Elizabeth assists and encourages the virgin mother. The virgin mother supports and keeps her aged cousin company. Their respective sons keep their own kind of supernatural connection alive, becoming interiorly attuned, as it were, for the lives and missions that are to unfold before them. The divine synergy is as high as it is deep in the household of Zechariah. Zechariah, like us, is mute before the Mystery taking place before his eyes. All of us are wordless in our apprehension of Mary's visitation with her cousin, Elizabeth. At a human level, they need each other; at a deeper, more supernatural level, however, they are brought together by the Incarnation of Mary's Son.

As human beings we also need each other. Yet, our deepest bonds – the bonds that make lifelong friends and endure unto eternity – stem from those forged in the blood of the Lamb who is slain (Rev. 5:6). "Do not think that I have come to bring peace to the earth; I have not come to bring peace, but a sword. For I have come to set a man against his father, and a daughter against her mother, and a daughter-in-law against her mother-in-law; and one's foes will be members of one's own household. Whoever loves father or mother more than me is not worthy of me; and whoever loves son or daughter more than me is not worthy of me" (Mt. 10:34-37). Supernatural ties trump merely human ones. Bonds of affection forged "in Christ" supersede and outlast all those based only on natural considerations, even while enriching "whatever is true, honorable, just, pure, and worthy of praise" in our relationships with others (Phil. 4:8).

We see in Mary's Visitation with Elizabeth the divine "togetherness" that Jesus brings. He comes to restore the Original Unity lost in the Fall of Adam and Eve.[83] He is the 2nd Adam, Mary the 2nd Eve, recapitulating and restoring what our first parents forfeited with their sin. Wherever they go, the Restoration occurs. We see in the Visitation a prelude, as it were, to the universal restoration of brotherhood that is afforded when the Son of God become man. It is the Fatherhood of God that ensures the brotherhood of man.[84] The instrument for this divine assurance is the Incarnation of His Son. The divinely chosen God-bearer (*Theotokos*) of our Salvation is Mary, his mother. As she brings Jesus to Elizabeth and Zechariah in Judea, we see in a preliminary way how the entire world will be delivered from its brokenness and dissolution. Jesus in the womb of Mary: the Divine Wisdom, creating holy communion wherever He is received, forging bonds of undying love wherever He and his mother are accepted. The wordless love of Mary and Elizabeth is an image and instance of what is given to all who know Him whom Mary brings.

---

[83] "Original unity" is the term used by Pope John Paul II to describe the paradisal state of perfect communion of human persons prior to the condition of sin. See John Paul II, *Man and Woman He Created Them: A Theology of the Body*, 156-157.

[84] As Pope Benedict XVI was fond of saying, "The fatherhood of God gives Christian brotherhood its firm foundation." *The Meaning of Christian Brotherhood*, 45.

Nativity

"But as he considered this, behold, and an angel of the Lord appeared to him in a dream, saying, 'Joseph, son of David, do not fear to take Mary as your wife; for that which is conceived in here is of the Holy Spirit.'"

The mystery of the Nativity opens with Joseph wrestling with his fears. He is torn. The virgin Mary is with child. Yet, she is but a child herself. It makes no sense. There is nothing about her that bespeaks anything other than purity and beauty. She is innocent. Joseph knows this in his heart. Still, she is "with child." How can this be? In asking this question, Joseph stands somewhere between Mary and her uncle, Zechariah, who asked the same question, "How can this be?" when given the unlikely news that they would be parents (Lk. 1:13). In this, Joseph resembles us who know ourselves to be not as saintly as Mary yet wanting to be less skeptical than Zechariah.

For the moment, Joseph is stuck in the realm of reason and psychology. He is trying to work things out in his mind, using reason alone. Presumably he falls asleep from exhaustion. We too eventually grow tired whenever we try to control life in our minds.

Then, *"behold, an angel of the Lord appeared to him..."* A dream from on high descends upon him. It gathers him up into a realm higher than his mind. It illumines his imagination with a different vision of Mary, of what she is being asked to do. Heavenly wisdom must always overshadow and illumine human reasoning if the truth of any situation is to be perceive in its proper depth. This is what is given to Joseph in his dream. His mind is elevated and infused by a kind of knowledge that surpasses that which he could conjure up on his own. The messenger of God gives Joseph to understand that *"that which is conceived of Mary is of the Holy Spirit."* We imagine the exhalation Joseph breathes even in his sleep! His anxiety is dispelled. He sleeps like a baby, even though he himself is probably old enough to be Mary's grandfather.

Recall that Joseph is a *"son of David."* He is an heir of the promise (Gen. 12:7; cf. Rom. 4:13). He is one in line with those from between whose legs the mace of kingly rule is said never to depart (Gen. 49:10). He is a descendent of the one to whom the covenant was made that the fidelity of the Lord would be unfailing (2 Sam. 7:13-16); that "even if we are unfaithful, God is faithful, for He cannot deny Himself" (2 Tim. 2:13). Was Joseph conscious of all this? Did he know in his bones that the Kingdom promised to his father, David, "would endure for all generations" (2 Sam. 7:24-27)? Was he a man of optimism and hope based on the sure and certain faith that the God of Israel would make good on His assurances to his servant, David? The Fathers of the Church believed so. They "interpreted his intention not as an attitude of suspicion but as a sign that he realized that God was the cause of what had happened."[85]

In any event, the angel says to Joseph, *"Do not fear,"* aware, perhaps, that Joseph is only human, that even his knowledge of God's promises does not guarantee his unwavering trust. For faith is always a gift, even for Joseph. It always requires a special grace to keep it alive. Faith is like a cactus in the desert. It is a hardy and tenacious plant, yet it still needs water. God sends his angel to Joseph in the desert of his fear, doubt, and insecurity to provide the few drops of nocturnal dewfall that will enable Joseph to arise refreshed in his understanding of God's mysterious fidelity.

Joseph is to *"take Mary as your wife; for that which is conceived in her is of the Holy Spirit."*

Jesus is the ultimate reason Joseph's fears are to be dispelled. Indeed, Jesus is the answer to every human fear. "Be not afraid!" was Christ's refrain to those who would take up their cross and follow Him (Jn. 6:20; 14:27), both before and after His Resurrection (Mt.

---

[85] *Navarre Bible,* note on Mt. 1:18-25.

28:5). But Joseph knows none of this yet. All is still enshrouded in mystery for him. He has the assurances of the angel. He hears a promise about the Holy Spirit. He is asked to move forward in faith. He takes consolation in the announcement of the Mystery.

We notice as a sidebar here that husband and wife are most deeply bonded by the promise of a child. In the case of Joseph and Mary, of course, that child is Jesus, Savior of the world. But, for any marriage, openness to children and openness to Jesus are pre-requisites for a true nuptial union. Without such openness, the couple is turned in upon themselves. Their "union" never rises much beyond an arrangement of utility. Their "marriage" devolves into an exercise in mutual manipulation, even if that manipulation wears the happy face of mutual satisfaction. Pleasure is not purpose. And life has very little purpose if Christ and children are not somehow at the heart of it.

"That which is conceived" in Mary, the angel tells Joseph, *"is of the Holy Spirit."*

Herein is contained an infinity of divine and human truth. Jesus is both God and man. His Father is God, His mother is Mary. This is the meaning of the angel's words. He is bone of Mary's bone, flesh of Mary's flesh. He is "conceived *in* her." Yet, *"that which* is conceived" is *"of* the Holy Spirit. The Mystery of Christ is the Mystery of the Eternal Word. Jesus, now the son of Mary, is also the Son of God – the Second Person of the Blessed and Immortal Holy Trinity. This is the meaning of the phrase, *"of* the Holy Spirit": Jesus is (as the Council of Chalcedon would later put it) "God from God, Light from Light, true God from true God, consubstantial with the Father, eternally begotten, never made." The entire Mystery of the Incarnation – and even of the Trinity – is contained in these few words communicated to Joseph in a dream.

There is also something very significant in the awkward-sounding phrase *"that which* is conceived in her." It almost makes Jesus sound like a "thing," an object placed in the womb of Mary for an instrumental purpose that will only become clear later. Nothing could be further from the truth. Jesus is neither an object nor an instrument, nor is Mary a mere means to anything other than her identity as mother of the Son of God and the Son of Man. These instrumentalist views of Jesus and Mary grieve the Holy Spirit. The Mystery of the Incarnation far transcends any mechanical model we might be tempted to use to describe it. Jesus is *the* Mystery before which all purely instrumental systems dissolve. Human reason can neither contain nor adequately describe Who He is or what He has come to accomplish. He is "before all else that is" (Col. 1:17). He is conceived "of the Holy Spirit." Explanatory narratives of mythology or metaphysics can never capture who He is or what He is all about. "I come from the Father and return to the Father" (Jn. 16:28; cf. 13:3). The Mystery of Jesus as the only-begotten Son of God can be truly glimpsed or accounted for by the canons of human logic. Jesus is the Standard without other standards. He is the criteria-less Criterion. He is the *sui generis* Key Hypothesis. He is the Rule and Measure of every other truth. There are no alternative schemas of truth that can ever adequately "explain" Jesus.

Truth and Person are synonymous in Jesus. He Himself *is* the Truth (Jn. 14:6). He is the Divine Truth that precedes all other truths. Human truth does exist. Human reason can attain to the truth. Yet, at bottom, all human reason, all human logic, all human thirst for and acquisition of truth is a function of – and reflection of – Jesus Himself. He is the Divine *Logos* who provides structure and light to all that exists. Jesus is the Only-begotten Son of God. It is from Him – the Primordial and Eternal Word of the Father – that all words and grammars, all syntax and logic, derive their coherence. He is the invisible Glue that holds together everything we see and are given to know. He is the Divine Logic that "explains" all that is seen and unseen (Col. 1:16). Jesus is the Truth for which both scientists and poets, theologians and philosophers seek. He is *"that"* Mystery which is conceived *"in* Mary" *"of* the Holy Spirit."

> *"She will bear a son, and you shall call his name Jesus,*
> *for he will save his people from their sins."*

"Jesus," "Son," and "Savior" come together in "*that* Mystery" "conceived in Mary" "of the Holy Spirit." Salvation is not primarily something Jesus brings. It is the Someone He is. He bears in His own Person the Kingdom of God. More properly put: He is *Autobasileia:* the Kingdom of God present in the flesh. He gathers around Himself the lost tribes of Israel. He Himself is the "light unto the nations" that Israel was meant to be (cf. Isa. 42:6; 49:6). Communion with Him constitutes salvation. He is the Grace and Truth, Peace and Promise of God. Union with Him is the content of salvation.

It is very difficult to get our minds and hearts around the truth that "to be saved" is not merely a matter of receiving something from God, even "the forgiveness of our sins." Salvation goes far deeper than any commercial or forensic ideas of it. It involves something fundamentally more primordial. "Salvation" consists in receiving *a real share* in the divinity of Christ. Salvation means to be "brought into" and receive a "participation in" His Sonship with the Father. In Jesus we become "partakers of the divine nature" (2 Pt. 1:4). We are made one with Him in His Trinitarian identity. The Trinitarian dimensions of Jesus' Name precede His soteriological power as our Deliverer. "Jesus" means, literally, "Yahweh saves." Yahweh is the Father of Jesus and Jesus is Yahweh's Only-begotten Son. To be saved is to receive an engrafting – an assimilation or "assumption" – into the Person of Jesus. We become sharers in His eternally unique, incomparably singular communion with the Father and the Holy

Spirit. "Salvation" is our insertion into the perichoretic love of the Most Blessed Trinity.

Recall also how throughout Scripture, "naming" is an act of re-creation (e.g. Gen. 17:5, 15; 32:28; Mt. 16:18). Adam is given power by God to "name" the plants and animals of the earth (Gn. 2:28). In so doing he "acquires dominion over them." To know someone's name is to know their secret. A person's unique identity is mysteriously contained and concealed in his or her name. God re-names Abram to Abraham when He "re-creates" him from being a wandering Armenian into "the father of many nations" (Gen. 17:5). The angel of the Lord re-names Jacob Israel when he re-configures him with a limp "for you have striven with God and with men, and have prevailed" (Gn. 32:19). Saul is re-named Paul when he is given his mission as "apostle to the Gentiles," and it is revealed to him "how much he will have to suffer in My (Jesus') Name" (Acts 9:16). Name = Power. Power = Purpose. "Jesus" = "Salvation." To be baptized "into the Name of Jesus" is to be assimilated into His mission as Redeemer of the world. It is to receive a participation in His processional identity as Son in the Father's Embrace through the Power of the Holy Spirit. This is our re-creation, this is our Redemption, this is our Salvation. Hence, "Jesus" is the Name "above every other names" (Eph. 1:21). "No other name is given under heaven by which we can be saved" (Acts 4:12). In Jesus "the power of God's Name" achieves its full re-creative impact.[86]

---

[86] See Alphonse and Rachel Goettmann, *The Power of the Name: The History and Practices of the Jesus Prayer.*

$\mathscr{M}$atthew 1:22-23

"All this took place to fulfill what the Lord has spoken by the prophet, 'Behold, a virgin shall conceive and bear a son, and his name shall be called Emmanuel' (which means, God with us)."

Something momentous is happening in the conception of Jesus History itself is reaching its climax, its culmination. All the forces of nature and grace are coming together – holding their collective breath, as it were – for what is coming in Jesus. There is a cosmic re-alignment, a universal rectification. Israel's prophets have predicted this for centuries. They have appeared on the world stage as messengers from God – His heralds, functioning more powerful than Paul Revere as they shouted out, "The Savior is coming! The Savior is coming!" Isaiah, Jeremiah, Ezekiel; Micah, Zechariah, Habakkuk: these prophets of God had the deepest, dimmest premonitions of Yahweh's messianic Deliverer. Yet, their writing give us no clear consensus on the form or content, time or manner of His advent or program. Here Isaiah speaks of "a virgin conceiving and bearing a son." Is this the Son of Man foreseen by Daniel (Dan. 7:13)? Or is this the many-eyed Phantom envisioned by Ezekiel (Ezek. 1:18)? Jesus is completely in the dark until the Spirit reveals Him as the Light of the World (Jn. 8:12; 9:5) and the Lamb of God (Jn. 1:29, 36). Yet, even when He appears in the world, the world will not received Him. "He was in the world, and the world was made through Him, yet the world knew Him not. He came to His own and his own received Him not…for people loved darkness rather than light because their deeds were evil…But to all who received Him,

107

who believe in His Name, He gave the power to become children of God" (Jn. 1:10-11; 3:19; 1:12).

Jesus fulfills the prophets, but He also exceeds them. He confounds, in the excess of His kenotic glory, the sum and substance of all their predictions. He bursts the categories of their legal and commercial systems. He is New Wine uncontainable by their old wineskins (Mt. 9:17). The Law cannot constrain Him. He embodies the Law but blows it asunder at the same time.

Jesus is everything the prophets predict but in a Form they do not expect. Like the light of the Resurrection itself, their eyes cannot comprehend what – Who – they are beholding. He is a *Someone*, not a something. In His very flesh He is beyond what any of them have foreseen. His limitedness is infinitely upsetting to them. They are blinded by the softness of His light. He is "God-with-us" (Emmanu-el), but not in a manner they can understand. His very rationality is irrational to them. As Logos-made-visible, He makes no sense to them. They expect a word from God, to be sure; they do not expect the Word-made-flesh.

Jesus is the Eternal Word of the Father. He is the Son of God in heaven and the Son of Man on earth. His very flesh is the Father's speech. Jesus and His Father are one (Jn. 10:30). Yet, the Father is greater than He (Jn. 14:28). The Father is the Speaker. Jesus is the Spoken. Their Spirit is the Breath with which He is spoken and heard. All this occurs simultaneously. All is inseparably conjoined. Yet each Person is indivisibly distinct. Each is completely different. And it is this Trinitarian glory that the Son has come to reveal. And not simply to reveal. To manifest, to show forth, to impart. To bequeath. To offer a "sharing in" for those He has come to deliver.

He comes to deliver us from sin and disobedience and death. From our slavery to self-service and self-satisfaction. He comes to deliver us into His Kingdom of Light and Peace and Joy. He comes to bring us into the Kingdom of His Father. He comes to incorporate us into the Embrace of Father, Son, and Spirit.

Only a virgin is fitting enough for the advent of Him who is God-with-us. For if only "the pure of heart shall see God" (Mt. 5:8), how much more so must it be the case that only the pure of heart and body should be counted worthy to conceive of God in the womb? It is no misguided pristine or Manichean piety that believes this. It is the "fittingness" of the *Economia* that matters here, not mere physicality. For God is a God of order. Not the obsessive-compulsive rigidity of the religiously self-righteous, but the humble, simple, clean, and unassuming orderliness embodied by Mary and Joseph in Nazareth. Like Mary's parents before them, Mary and Joseph had no children. But, unlike Joachim and Ann (as well as the other fruitless couples in the old covenant who saw barrenness as a curse), Mary and Joseph revered Mary's virginity as an icon of divine promise. Hers was a holy, virginal receptivity. Her holy desire constituted an ovulation of faith most attractive to the Holy Spirit. For those who have eyes to see, Mary's perpetual virginity is the portrait of perfect fruitfulness. So attractive is she to God that He inseminates her with His very Life. In her – Virgin and Mother – the Son of God assumes human nature in the flesh and becomes the Son of Man, Emmanuel, God-with-us.

"In those days a decree went out from Caesar Augustus that all the world should be enrolled....And so Joseph also went up from Galilee, from the city of Nazareth, to Judea, to the city of David, which is called Bethlehem, because he was of the house and lineage of David, to be enrolled with Mary his betrothed, who was with child."

"In those days..."

It is *chronos*, not *kairos*, time being spoken of here: time experienced as two-dimensionl, as a flat line, as something sequential, something inexorable, something naturalistic, mechanistic. Something 'moving ahead,' grinding underneath everyone and everything it encompasses. Time as a totalitarian behemoth, governed by impersonal and naturalistic 'laws,' the world and realm of political power. This is the experience of history as unredeemed, history as not yet illuminated by the Light from on high (cf. Lk. 1:78).

"Caesar Augustus published a decree..."

Caesar issues a secular *fiat*: "Let it be done according to *my* will"...the opposite (anti-type) to the fiat of Mary: "Let it be done *to me* according to *Your* will." Self-assertion as opposed to self-surrender. Human assertiveness untempered by knowledge of God, self-assertion unredeemed by the grace of Christ. Self-will run riot. Self-importance writ large on the world stage. The natural disposition of the rulers and principalities of this world, fueled and fostered by the powers and principalities of the world below (cf. Rom. 8:38; Eph. 3:10; 6:12; Col. 1:16; 2:15). Unbeknownst to Caesar, he is but the puppet of the Prince of this world (Eph. 2:2, 22; cf. Mt. 12:24) who furnished him with the impetus to move forward with his grandiose scheme.

"...ordering a census of the whole world..."

No one escapes the calculations of Caesar. No one exceeds the long reach of the totalitarian state. No one escapes the machinations of the political class, puppets though they be of powers more infernal than themselves. In their view, people are only numbers, data in a census. Persons "count" only to the degree that they can be used for something, only for what they can do for the ruling class. Usefulness is the only criterion. Utilitarianism, pragmatism, relativism: these are the only "dogmas" [anti-dogmas, really] employed by the purveyors of the census. These are the only "truths' permitted under the dictatorship of relativism. And they desire to "count" in order to "know." For as with all Gnostics, knowledge is power, information an instrument of coercion. And power is for the purposes of self-aggrandizement. There is no room in this climate for the dignity of the individual person. Persons count only as numbers. They are statistics, data, nameless entities on a pre-modern spreadsheet. For Caesar, as for political powers before and since, people exist to be used for the ruler's purposes, pure and simple. This side of God's grace, no earthly ruler naturally desires to serve the persons identified in his or her census.

"And so Joseph went to Judea, to David's town of Bethlehem..."

Joseph is the obedient citizen, the model citizen. Yet, he is a citizen of two worlds: the world of God and the world of Caesar. Quite naturally, without the benefit of his Son's later instruction, Joseph "renders unto Caesar what is Caesar's" (Lk. 10:25) while rendering unto God what belongs exclusively to Him. In this Joseph anticipates not only what Jesus would later teach about his follower's attitude towards church and state, but what the *Letter to Diognetes*, the *Apology* of Justin Martyr, and the testimony of the saints throughout the history of the Church insist upon, namely that good citizenship in the Kingdom of God makes for responsible citizenship in the legitimate kingdoms of this world (cf. Rom. 13). "Seek ye first the Kingdom of God and all these other things will be given you as well" (Mt. 6:33). If we seek first the kingdom of God and make the love of God our first priority, we will also acquire a connatural sense of the rights and responsibilities of our civic duty. Not only is Christian faith no threat to the social and political orders of this world, it is their only guarantee. Though far from the thoughts of Joseph as he sets out for Judea, these truths are evident in his humble, spontaneous, obedient, supremely self-possessed compliance with the despot's order.

Joseph goes from one small town (Nazareth) to another (Bethlehem). He is always in the shadows, out of the limelight. No big city lights for Joseph and Mary. They prefer the hidden life, the village life, the life of peaceful anonymity, nestled safely in the strong, invisible arms of God. Did Joseph contemplate the prophet Micah's words as he journeyed towards Judea: *"But you, O Bethlehem of Ephrathah, who are one of the little clans of Judah, from you shall come forth for me one who is to rule in Israel, whose origin is from of old, from ancient days"* (Mic. 5:2)? Bethlehem, of course, is "David's town," not the "City of David" (Jerusalem). Bethlehem is the birthplace and childhood town of David the shepherd. Joseph is traveling towards the town of David the child, David the giant-killer, not David the king, not the David who is like unto Caesar, not David the adulterer and murderer, intoxicated with political power and full of himself unto his own spiritual and political downfall. Joseph is en route to the town of the apolitical David, the pre-political David; to the David as first seen by the prophet Saul who discerned in him the child-like beauty that imaged forth divine power (1 Sam. 16:12-14).

Bethlehem is also the "House of Bread." Here it is, lying in a manger – a feeding trough for animals – that the Bread of Life will first offer Himself to the world for the life of the world (Jn. 6:51). But these thoughts are hidden from Joseph at this stage in his journey. He goes to Bethlehem simply *"...because he was of the house and lineage of David to register with Mary, his espoused wife, who was with child..."*

In this Joseph was, at one level, simply doing his civic duty, though at great inconvenience and expense to him and his family. Was Mary expected to come along? Was she required to accompany him, given her maternal condition? Could Joseph have registered without her? These questions become irrelevant once we realize that everything Joseph and Mary did related not to civic duty but to their promptings from the Holy Spirit. Joseph – ever since being inspired to present himself in his dotage as a Spirit-inspired suitor for the maiden from Nazareth – does nothing without Mary. He is completely dedicated (wedded) to her, despite the fact that, technically speaking, they are only "espoused." He is fully committed. He is the model of perfect fidelity. And, as the man in her life, Joseph is, in God's plan, a *sine quo non* of the Theo-drama about to played out in the cave in Bethlehem. In other words, Joseph is, and remains, as integral to Mary as Mary is to Jesus in the Mystery of salvation. He is no accidental appendage to her divine maternity, just as Mary herself is no incidental incubation chamber for the birth of the Redeemer. The Mystery is altogether personal, and the persons involved (Joseph and Mary) are absolutely essential to what is transpiring in all its contingency and holy irreducibility. We will never know what dangers, obstacles, or challenges Joseph and Mary encountered on their way to Judea. To be sure, every step of the journey was fraught with ominous possibilities. The very lack of detail in the narrative gives witness to Joseph's solid protection, his silent strength. He is revealed in the story as model husband and protector. Joseph and Mary belong together, not only as spouses in the Lord but as icons of the Trinitarian love that their Son is about to manifest to the world.

The focus now shifts to their child. Joseph, as is his wont, slips quietly into the background. The gospel simply says Mary "was with child." How unassuming a biblical description leading up to what is about to transpire! For Mary's child is the epicenter of the drama. He is the reason there are any Scriptures at all. All now is in readiness. The prophets' words are about to be fulfilled. The virgin is about to gift the world with Emmanuel (Isa. 7:14). He will be born in the little, humble, unremarkable town of Bethlehem. The Nativity is upon us! O silent night!

$\mathcal{L}$uke 2:6-7

"While they were there the time came for her to be delivered. She gave birth to her first-born son and wrapped him in swaddling clothes and laid him in a manger..."

Mary's "confinement" is at an end. The Word of God cannot be chained. Both Mary and her Son are the "hidden ones," the humble ones whose 'confinement" in obscurity cannot last forever. The Word of God germinates in silence, and Mary is the Woman of Silence. Yet, the Word of God is not forever silent. As the prophet Malachi said earlier and Simeon and Anna will soon discover, "... the Lord whom you seek will *suddenly* come to his temple..." (Mal. 3:1). Or as the Book of Wisdom puts it, "For while gentle silence enveloped all things, and night in its swift course was now half gone, your all-powerful word leapt from heaven, from the royal throne, into the midst of the land that was doomed..." (Wis. 18:14-15).

The Advent of the Lord is always discontinuous with human expectations. It is always "abrupt" in the sense of disorienting us with its inscrutable form and providential timing. It is always greater, always more than, always better than what we might have predicted or imagined. Once He appears everything in the world appears with Him in an altogether different light...a better light...a brighter light...yet, a Light to which – to Whom – the eyes of the world are still just beginning to become adjusted.

One phase of His new creation has now been completed. Mary's confinement, and Jesus' confinement within Mary's confinement has ended. A joyous birth is about to take place. This note of expectation echoes the birth of Esau and Jacob of Rebekah (Gen. 25:24),

115

and more recently that of the Baptist of Elizabeth (Lk. 1:57). This is
an exceedingly exciting phrase of anticipation: *"The time came for her to
be delivered"*. Jesus' birth recapitulates and exceeds all of the important
birth accounts in the Old Dispensation that gave expression to God's
undying fidelity to His chosen son, Israel (Lk. 1:50, 54) who "has
remembered His mercy forever."

How unassuming is the eight-word description of the salvation
of the world: *"And she gave birth to her first-born son..."*! This is perfectly
in keeping with both the grandeur and simplicity of the truth about
Jesus. For He Himself is "the Way, the Truth, and the Life (Jn. 14:6);
and, though it is true that "if all the things that Jesus did...were written down... the world itself could not contain the books that would
be written" (Jn. 21:25), it is also true that precisely because He is God
– whose greatest glory is manifest in His humility, whose divinity is
hypostatically and invisibly united to his humanity – everything that
can be said of the Lord is also contained in sum in these few simple
words. It takes but the eyes of faith to discern hidden within these
few words regarding the birth of Mary's *"first-born son"* the entirety of
"the Mystery hidden since the foundation of the world" (Eph. 3:9).

It is unworthy of us, is it not, to engage apologetically in defense of the phrase *"first born-son"*? All must be read "from above,"
not "from below." Jesus, the Eternal Word, is *first and foremost* "the
first-born Son of the Father" (Jn. 1:18; Col. 1:15). This description
implies neither subordination nor subsequent Sonship in the Life
of the Trinity. Jesus is the *Prototokos*: the "First Born" both of His
heavenly Father and His earthly mother. "First born," then, is a term
of *Trinitarian and Christological pre-eminence*, affirming and illuminating
Jesus' incomparable redemption role in the Father's Plan for the
world (Rom. 8:29; Col. 1:15; Heb. 1:6; Rev. 1:5). From an anagogical
perspective – which is the only standpoint we may devoutly assume
when contemplating the Nativity of Jesus – the use of this seemingly
banal term underlines the absolutely unique status and role of Jesus
in the redemption of the world. It refers not at all to other presumed

children of Mary. Such is a presumption can only be made by those unaware or hostile to the Tradition of the Church. Such opinions deserve no attention in our contemplation of the Incarnation.

In her humility and poverty, and in the biting cold of the Bethlehem night, the Ever-Virgin Mary *"wrapped him in swaddling clothes and laid him in a manger..."* She binds Him against the elements. She does so to protect Him, yet the swaddling clothes are also a sign of his imprisonment by Caiaphas and his execution at the hands of Pontius Pilate and the Jews. For Jesus is a slave to death in order to give us life. He is as immobile on the Cross as He is inseparable from His Father's love. In His Incarnation, these twin mysteries are the same. The form of His earth-bound love is to be wrapped in the straightjacket of suffering and death in order to bring life to the world. He not only cannot escape these 'swaddling clothes' but he desires not to do so. He assumes and is inexorably bound to our human nature in order to make of us "partakers" in His divine communion with the Father (2 Pt. 1:4).

Here we begin to perceive the co-redemptive suffering of the Mother with the Son. She seeks only to give comfort to her Holy Infant; yet, she can do so only in conformity with the pre-determined shape of the Son's obedience to the Father's Will. The shape of divine love is cruciform. The bonds that hold Jesus fast on the Cross are of a piece with the 'swaddling clothes' that bind him unmoving in the manger. Mary seeks to protect her Son, but is able to do so only in ways consonant with the larger Plan of Father and Son. She looks on Him with a certain helplessness. Mother and Son are held apart by the Holy Spirit just as Father and Son are held apart by the Holy Spirit in the Paschal Mystery. Jesus lays down His life for the life of the world (Jn. 6:51). He does so deliberately, intentionally, joyously (cf. Jn. 10:17-18; Heb. 12:2). He does so as the consummation of Trinitarian Love. Mary consents to this cruciform expression of divine love. She recognizes that the Mystery of divine *kenosis* is

always and forever identical with His being rendered helpless...
pinned down...'*wrapped in swaddling clothes.*'

He is also *"laid in a manger"* by His mother. The 'passivity' of
the divine Son of God in all of this is significant. He is "given to"
the world by His Father, and given as "food for the world" by His
mother. For here He is, "laid in a manger" – an eating trough for
animals – in "Bethlehem" – the House of Bread. Mary is the Mother
of the Eucharist far in anticipation of the Last Supper. And in the
Eucharist, Jesus extends and makes available to us a share in the
absolute humility with which He consents and designs to be "laid
in a manger" by His mother.

The "givenness" of Jesus – or, better, the "given-over-ness" –
remains an abiding, integral, defining quality of both His divine and
human Sonships. He is always the Begotten and Beholden One. He
is utterly *relational* in his identity as both God and man. He is *never
without* the ones who give Him to the world. He is "given over" by
both His Father and mother for the life of the world, even as He
"gives Himself over" without coercion for our salvation (cf. Jn.
18:36). He is forever the Divine Victim in a way that is paradoxically
yet hypostatically united to His eternal identity as our Great High
Priest (Heb. 2:17).

$\mathscr{L}$uke 2:8

"In that region there were shepherds living in the fields,
keeping watch over their flock by night."

Shepherds: the image of vigilance. Icons of simplicity, peace, watch-fulness, attentiveness...what the ascetical monks of the desert would later call *nepsis*: wakefulness of the heart, alert and sensitive to any movements in the middle of the night.

Shepherds are also men acquainted with silence. Nothing would surprise them, yet they are always prepared for the unexpected. They are alert but not apprehensive; on the lookout but not necessarily suspicious. They are calm and peaceful, yet careful and not naïve. They are also humble. Ultimately they do what they do for no other reason than they love their sheep. They certainly do not do if for the money. They are no hirelings (Jn. 10:12). They are Joseph-like in their silence and humility. They live behind the scenes, yet are utterly integral to the life and mission of God's Son. They live away from the limelight..."*in the fields,*" as it were, where the bright lights of the city cannot darken their understanding of what is transpiring before them. They are '*keeping watch over their flocks'* in the Dark Night guided only by the Living Flame of Love burning in their hearts.[87]

Because they live "in the heart," the shepherds have also learned to trust their instincts. They "trust their gut," as modern parlance has it. They listen and move based on their intuition, honed and

---

[87] As St. John of the Cross writes: "*One dark night,* fired with love's urgent longings - ah, the sheer grace! - I went out unseen, my house being now all stilled...On that glad night, in secret, for no one saw me, nor did I look at anything, *with no other light or guide than the one that burned in my heart...*" The Dark Night, 1, 3 (emphasis added).

119

refined by long years of vigilant experience. They are therefore existentially open to whatever might come their way. Their only agenda is to protect their sheep. They are simple men dedicated to defending ignorant animals. Yet, it this very Blessed Ignorance that Divine Wisdom would use to reveal His incarnate Glory. He would employ the image of the Good Shepherd as an abiding image of Himself, and He would identify as "sheep" those who would hear His voice and follow in His ways (Jn. 10:11-14). "Feed My sheep!" would be His final commission to those who would do His Will by serving as His vicars in the world (Jn. 21:15-17).

The shepherds are *"keeping watch over their flocks by night."* Does this mean they are the first to see the prophecy of Isaiah fulfilled: The people who walked in darkness have seen a great light; those who lived in a land of deep darkness--on them light has shined" (Isa. 9:2)? He always shows Himself to the humble, while the haughty find Him impossible to perceive (Lk. 1:52; cf. Prv. 3:34; 15:25; Jas. 4:6). He always satisfies the hungry, while the well-sated go without (Lk. 1:53; cf. Ps. 34:11; Prv. 10:3). He always appears in the darkness, the Light that cannot be overcome (Jn. 1:5). The shepherds are blessed with an Epiphany no less than the Wise Men who followed His star from the East (Mt. 2:1ff.).

$\mathcal{L}$uke 2:9-10a

"Then an angel of the Lord stood before them, and the glory of the Lord shone around them, and they were terrified. But the angel said to them, 'Do not be afraid...'"

Out of the blackness of the night, *"an angel of the Lord stands before them."* The appearance of the angel is calm, certain, sudden. We can only guess at the angel's 'physical' dimensions. Concomitant with the angelic appearance, *"the glory of the Lord shone around them..."* The divine *Kabod (דובכ)* envelops them. This divine illumination, as bright as it is, also has a certain heaviness, or gravitas, about it. It is, as St. Paul tells us, "the weight of glory" (2 Cor. 4:17). It presses down upon the shepherds. They feel like they are suffocating under the appearance of the angel. Their reaction is that of panic. *"They were terrified."* Perhaps in their paralysis, they provide us with a premonition of our own Particular Judgment, i.e., coming face-to-face with our Guardian Angel who will bring us to God?

In short order, however, they hear the reassuring words, *"Do not be afraid!"* These are of a piece with those of the One who sends the angel and whose birth the angel announces. For Jesus' frequent refrain to those overwhelmed by His Presence is "Be not afraid!" Peter hears these words as he falls at the feet of Jesus, overwhelmed by his own sinfulness in the wake of the Master's miracle (Lk. 5:8), and all the apostles hear these words when they fear for their lives in the Galilean storm (Mt. 8:25-27). The life of Jesus is book-ended by an angel's admonition, "Do not be afraid!" The angel at the tomb says the exact same thing as the angel of the Annunciation (Lk. 1:30;

121

Mt. 28:5). Jesus, too, especially after His Resurrection, reassures us in His glory: "Peace be with you!" (Jn. 20:19, 21, 26; Lk. 24:36).

We are struck, finally, by the dispassionate tenor of the angel's participation in, and conveyance of, the Lord's heavenly glory. Angels regard our sins with indifference, and they account our emotional reactions, if not odd, at best incidental to what they have come to say and do.[88] The only thing that matters to them is their message, and our response to their message. Once that is secured, their mission is finished. Angels are God's messengers. Faithful from all eternity, they share in, and serve to make manifest, the glory of the One they serve. They appear to human persons simply to deliver a Word of the Lord. Once their mission is accomplished, they return from whence they came. They are the epitome of humility, even if their appearance overwhelms the shepherds with the weight of God's glory.

The appearance of angels (Gen. 16:7-13; Ex. 3:24-; 14:19; Jdg. 6:11-22; Hos. 12:4-5) signals the actual presence of God himself (cf. Ex. 16:10; 24:16-17; 29:43; 40:34-35; Lev. 9:6; Num. 14:10; 16: 19, 42; 20:6; 1 Kg. 8:11; Ps. 138:5; Isa. 58:8; Ezek. 1:28; Tob. 12:15). Perhaps the most famous of such appearances is the visitation of the three angels – disguised as mortal "travelers" – who appear to Abraham under the oaks of Mamre (Gen. 18:1-15). This "Old Testament Trinity," as it is sometimes called and pictured,[89] prefigures these angelic interventions that signal the appearance of the actual Trinity in history through event of Jesus' Incarnation.

---

[88] St. John of the Cross notes that "the angels who judge perfectly the things that give sorrow without the feeling of sorrow, and exercise the works of mercy without the feeling of compassion." *Spiritual Canticle*, XX. 10.

[89] The Church has many depictions of the Holy Trinity, but the icon which most profoundly reflects the Trinitarian Mystery is that of the Orthodox saint and iconographer, Andrei Rublev (136—1428). His 'Old Testament Trinity' depicts the Trinity in the form of three angels. The prototype for this icon was the mysterious appearance of the Holy Trinity in the form of three travelers to Abraham and Sarah under the oak of Mamre. The Church recognizes this as perhaps the most beautiful icon ever 'written' because it most fully gives expression to the dogma of the Holy Trinity: the three angels are depicted in equal dignity, symbolizing the *triunity and*

$\mathcal{L}$uke 2:10b-11

"And the angel said to them, '...behold, I bring you good news of a great joy which will come to all the people; for to you is born this day in the city of David a Savior, who is Christ the Lord.'"

The gospel is good news. It is a proclamation of *great joy*. Pope Francis entitled his first encyclical, ***Evangelii Gaudium,*** The Joy of the Gospel. His pontificate is testimony to the overflowing joy that erupts in heaven the day Jesus is born into our world. It is an excess of heavenly joy that impels the angels to appear in the sky announcing the good news of the advent of the Redeemer. Mary, of course, "pondered these things in her heart" (Lk. 2:19; 51), and was enrapt in the joy of the gospel long before the outbursts of the angels. Though silent in Mary, the *Gloria in excelsis Deo* echoed triumphantly in the firmament over Bethlehem when He who came to re-create the universe first appeared in the manger as a defenseless, newborn infant.

Knowledge of Him is *"a great joy that will come to all the people..."*

Yes, Jesus is the Uncontainable One, and the difference He makes in the world is equally uncontainable. On Calvary He will become the Seed that "will fall to the ground and die" (Jn. 12:24), but whose fruitfulness will be without limitation. Through Him, with Him, and in Him, all things will be restored and redeemed. The world will not simply be refurbished and divested of the grime and sin that overlay its original beauty, but it will be elevated and

---

equality of all three Persons. For an in-depth explanation of the various dimensions and mystical symbolism of the Rublev icon, see: http://www.sacredheartpullman. org/Icon%20explanation.htm.

perfected in ways unimaginable to the fallen mind that can conceive of creation only in limited, utilitarian terms.

The moment Jesus enters the world, the world changes forever. Henceforth history will be the progressive, if mysterious and hidden (cf. Mk. 4:27; Mt. 25:3), unfolding of the Kingdom of God. This Kingdom has come in the flesh in the Person of Jesus. He is a Divine Pebble, plopped by the Father into the pond of His infinitely expanding universe. His Incarnation and Paschal Mystery have triggered a tidal way of uncontainable re-creative Energy throughout the universe. The consequences of His appearance among us are as incomprehensible as they are inspiring. The Last Days of the world have been set in motion by the first day of Jesus. No one can comprehend what lies ahead. Yet, those "assimilated into Christ" who have in themselves "the mind that was in Christ" (1Cor. 2:16; Phil. 2:5) can rejoice in the knowledge that "as the rain and the snow come down from heaven, and return not thither but water the earth, making it bring forth and sprout, giving seed to the sower and bread to the eater, so shall my word be that goes forth from my mouth [Jesus], it shall not return to me empty, but shall accomplish that which I purpose, and prosper in the thing for which I sent it." (Isa. 55:10–11). The gospel of joy - the confidence of the recapitulation and recreation of all things "in Christ" - is a universal joy. It includes the whole of creation as well as all nations on earth. It is cosmic in reach. Because of His appearance in the world, even "the very stones cry out" with joy (Lk. 19:40).

Jesus leads us towards an anagogical Catholicism: a vision of the Last Things that is not frightening in its unlimited scope but is truly awe-inspiring.[90] "Perfect love casts out all fear," Jesus tells us (1 Jn. 4:18). The Face of Jesus, appearing for the first time in that stable in Bethlehem, is the smile of the Father's perfect love upon our world of violence and death. He brings into our world a joy of Divine Discontinuity. He offers the world an invitation of an unimaginable

---

[90] See my book, *Deified Vision: Towards an Anagogical Catholicism.*

future in Him. His promises are meant to inspire hope and love, not fear or trepidation. "Fear not, little flock," He tells His disciples, "for it is your Father's good pleasure to give you the kingdom" (Lk. 12:32). The future Jesus offers us is as incomprehensibly good as He is Himself. He is the one whom death could not contain (cf. Acts 2:24). The promise and power He implants in our world enables the world to exceed itself. In and through Jesus, all nations will see the glory of God. This is an eschatological expectation, not an apocalyptic threat. It is joy, not trepidation, that follows the appearance of Jesus. He comes forever as the Redeemer, casting judgment upon no one (Jn. 8:15), and delivering back to the Father all things recapitulated in His Divine Love.

"...to you is born this day..."

Jesus is God-with-us, Emmanuel. It pleases Him - no, Eternal Love compels Him - to make His dwelling, to pitch His tent among sinful human persons. He is "turned towards" the Father in the Trinity (Jn. 1:1) and "towards us" in His Incarnation.[91] His desire is to never be without us, just as His identity is to never be without His Father. Jesus is no Janus-faced Savior: He is not the two-faced monster of Christian kitsch Who shows condemnation one moment and forgiveness the next. On the contrary, He is the Incarnation of Divine Love that shows to the world the singular Face of Divine Mercy. He is turned towards His Father in perpetual adoration and thanksgiving, and He is turned towards us in infinite kindness and mercy. He is turned towards the Father of Mercy in heaven, and He is turned towards us in need of mercy in this earthly vale of tears.

For His Mercy to be effective, we must *receive* Him. He is given us by the Father in order to be received. Like a midwife catching a baby swiftly delivered, or like being offered an infant to hold, we

---

[91] Jn. 1:1: "The Word was with God" = "The Word was turned towards God" *(pros ton theon)*. Here we glimpse the God-ward posture of Jesus from all eternity, indicating a certain dialogical dimension within the Trinitarian Mystery itself.

must take Him in our arms and hold Him to ourselves if we are to benefit from His birth. For Jesus is a total Gift to us from above. "Divinity flew down to draw humanity up," wrote Ephrem the Syrian.[92] He descends into our world so that we might ascend with Him to the right hand of His Father. "God became man so we could become God."[93] This miracle of salvation, - this mystery of deification - cannot be ours unless we "let it be done to us according to His will" (Lk. 1:38).

It is again revealing that the Redeemer's advent into our world is first announced to the shepherds. Essentially outlaws, they were considered as trustworthy as modern-day gypsies. They were known to steal, cheat, lie, and do whatever necessary to perpetuate their marginalized style of life. Already Jesus is showing his desire to call sinners, not the righteous, to a new kind of life (Mk. 2:17; Mt. 9:13; Lk. 5:32). Already He is demonstrating His desire to associate with tax collectors and prostitutes (Mt. 9:10-11; 11:19). Already He is penetrating the highways and byways seeking out and desiring to save what is lost (Lk. 19:10). In calling the shepherds and being born in a cave, Jesus signals to the world that His mission is to go into the deepest, darkest corners of the earth searching for those who have fallen through its cracks. He desires to shine His Father's saving Light upon all who sit in darkness and the shadow of eternal death (Lk. 1:79; Mt. 4:16).

He is born for us *"this day."* Every day is a new beginning in the Light of Christ. He is hope Incarnate. "In Your Light we see light, O Lord" (Ps. 36:9; cf. 89:15). Jesus is the Eighth Day - the omni-present Sabbath of the Lord in whom we find "rest for our souls" (Mt. 11:29). He is never more than a hair's breath away. Through His Incarnation He entered our world; through His Resurrection and

---

[92] *C.Nis* 48:17-18. St. Ephrem also said, "He gave us divinity, we gave Him humanity" (*H. de Fid.* 5. 7). References found in Norman Russell's magisterial work, *The Doctrine of Deification in the Greek Patristic Tradition*, 322.

[93] St. Athanasius, *On the Incarnation*, 54. Cf. *Catechism of the Catholic Church*, 460.

Ascension He has embedded our world into His. Every fiber of creation is permeated by the Freshness of His Holy Spirit. Every increment of time and space affords and avenue of accessibility and availability to the New Day of the Lord. Every day is a new day in the Kingdom of God. There is nothing old, nothing stale in the Realm of the Trinity. Hope springs eternal in the lives of those engrafted into Christ. The Living Water that is a Wellspring of Worship in Him, and it becomes a River of Life when it is poured into and over us through the Mysteries of His Church.

Newness is what we are given when we are anointed with His Spirit. "Behold, I make all things new!," Jesus says (Rev. 21:5). In Him we are "born again" (Jn. 3:5). We become the "little children" made worthy of the Kingdom of heaven (Mt. 18:3; cf. Jn. 1:12). We are meant to experience our life in Christ with the same joy as that of a small Child coming down the stairs on Christmas morning. "This day" is the only day, as far as they, and we, are concerned. For Christmas is a never-ending day for those who know the Gift they receive in Christ. As the hymn Amazing Grace puts it: "When we've been there ten thousand years…we've no less days to sing His praise than when we've first begun."

> *"And suddenly there was with the angel a multitude of the heav-*
> *enly host praising God and saying, Glory to God in the high-*
> *est, and on earth peace among men with whom he is pleased!"*

The multitude of angels cannot stay away. If the angels rejoice in heaven "over one sinner who repents" (Lk. 15:7), how much more so must they rejoice when they behold the Redeemer being born among the men and women He came to save? Wherever the Eternal Word goes, so too go His angels. We think here of the divine liturgy. As the *Catechism of the Catholic Church* states:

> "In the earthly liturgy we share in a foretaste of that heavenly liturgy which is celebrated in the Holy City of Jerusalem toward which we journey as pilgrims, where Christ is sitting at the right hand of God, Minister of the sanctuary and of the true tabernacle. *With all the warriors of the heavenly army* we sing a hymn of glory to the Lord; venerating the memory of the saints, we hope for some part and fellowship with them; we eagerly await the Savior, our Lord Jesus Christ, until he, our life, shall appear and we too will appear with him in glory."[94]

Angels are mediators between us and the Trinitarian Persons. They maintain Jacob's Ladder (Gen. 28:12) for us, urging and accompanying us to ascend to that Kingdom where they minister

---

[94] CCC 1090, emphasis added; cf. 1137-1139.

unceasingly to "the Lamb who is slain" (Rev. 5:6). Knowing themselves to be perfectly fulfilled in their glorification of God, they desire the same for us. It is natural for them to continuously praise the Creator; would, they wish, that such praise would become second-nature for us also.

At a very fundamental level, the angels don't understand us. They cannot adequately grasp the covetousness that drives our sin. The float above both the vices and virtues that pock mark the economy of our earthly existence. Satan, it is said, envied God and therefore fell into the fires of hell. Hell is of anyone's own making who sees the Other as a rival and experiences alienation as a result. The good angels, who never made God their rival, can do nothing other than exalt Him to the highest heavens. They find it impossible, however, to empathize with us in our weakness, as does our Great High Priest (Heb. 4:15). He it is that was, for a short time, "made a little less than the angels" (Heb. 2:7, 9) so as to identify with our weakness and death, and raise us up to New Life in His Spirit.

In the desert, Jesus allows Himself to listen to all the lies and temptations of the devil so that He might shows us the way through them in fidelity to His Father's voice (Lk. 4:1-12). Jesus is the Peace of God given to us in a world torn apart by violence. Angels cannot give us that Peace, nor can they, like us, be deified by a living connection to Christ (cf. 2 Cor. 5:17; Gal. 6:15). Jesus alone can impart the "peace that passes all understanding" (Phil. 4:7). He delivers us from the swamp of this world's satanic violence, generated by covetousness and our insidious comparisons with others. The angels wish us "... *peace on earth...*" but only the incarnate God, lying as a defenseless infant in an animals feeding trough, can afford us this peace.

The peace of Christ rests upon *"men with whom he is pleased..."*

Who are they with whom Christ is pleased? They are those to whom the Father has granted it. "No one can come to me," Jesus tells us, "unless it is granted to them by my Father" (Jn. 6:65). It is the Father Himself who says, "This is my Beloved Son in whom I am well pleased" (Lk. 3:22; cf. Mt. 12:18; 17:5). It is the 'good pleasure' between the Father and the Son into which we are taken up when the gift of faith is given us. Faith is a gift. This mysterious predilection of God is impossible for the human mind to grasp. Without this gift it is impossible to please God (Heb. 11:6). Yet, all is utter gratuity in God, and it is by His utter gratuity that we come to experience His peace that comes to us from Him. As the recipients of the gift of faith, we can say with St. Paul, "Blessed be the God and Father of our Lord Jesus Christ, who has blessed us in Christ with every spiritual blessing in the heavenly places, even as he chose us in him before the foundation of the world, that we should be holy and blameless before him…to the praise of his glorious grace which he freely bestowed on us in the Beloved" (Eph. 1:3–6).

$\mathcal{L}$uke 2:16-17

"And they went with haste, and found Mary and Joseph, and the babe lying in a manger. And when they saw it, they understood what had been told them concerning this child."

The shepherds hastening to the stable remind us of Mary hastening to the home of Elizabeth following the Annunciation (Lk. 1:39). Hastening is always something we do when the truth from on high suddenly becomes clear to us. Touched by an angel - whether divine or human - we can't wait to tell others about what we have seen and heard. Urgency follows naturally upon inspiration. We think also in this context of Jesus' urgency to be alone with His Father following His Baptism by John in the Jordan. He saw the heavens open, the dove descend, and the Voice of His Father tell the world, "This is My Beloved Son in whom I am well pleased" (Mk. 1:11). The Spirit then "drove Him into the desert" (Mk. 1:12; Mt. 4:1). There Jesus would be tested by the Tempter (Lk. 4:2), His mission of faithfulness to the Father's salvific design "purified as gold in fire" (Sir. 2:5; Zech. 13:9; 1 Pt. 1:7). "I have a baptism to be baptized with; and how I am constrained until it is accomplished!" (Lk. 12:50). Jesus' whole life was a *hastening* towards the End for which He was born.

Hastening to the stable where Jesus was born, however, was just the beginning of the shepherds' conversion. Like a hare off to the races, they had no idea about what lay ahead for them. The announcement of the angels acts as a stimulus and a catalyst for them, but it does not ensure them of anything more. The adrenaline of their religious experience will need a clearer on-going focus to sustain itself over time.

This focus is discovered when they *found Mary and Joseph, and the babe lying in a manger."* Upon entering the stable, they behold, as it were, a Trinitarian tableau: Mary, the Spouse and of the Holy Spirit, Joseph, the divinely-chosen image of God the Father, and Jesus, the Incarnate Child of the Kingdom of God. This encounter is a "saturated event,"[95] i.e., it overwhelms our ability to fully comprehend or express it. There is an excess of goodness presented to to the world in this scene that can only be received, not manipulated or managed. It is a Mystery of overflowing beauty defying categorization and resisting all interpretation. Like the Resurrection of Jesus itself, it envelops the faithful who behold it with an inexhaustible significance that cannot be put into words. It is utterly transformative for those who have the "eyes to see" (Lk 10:23; cf. Jn 12:40; Rom. 11:8). For here we see the Innocence from on high. We see that the Kingdom of God is a participation in the defenselessness of a child. We catch a glimpse of that heart-melting space into which a person must enter to be made worthy of the Presence of God. Falling our our knees seems the only appropriate response to what we behold here in the stable. It is not for nothing that manger scenes at Christmas picture the shepherds, the Kings, and even the animals in various forms of adoration before Jesus in the company of His Holy Family. Further, the innocence and helplessness of this Child invites the adoring visitor to take Jesus to oneself. "Here, hold Him for a minute!" is something we can imagine Mary saying to all those who come to worship Him. Jesus as Savior, Mary as Co-Redemptrix, and ourselves as persons created to hold Jesus in our hands and our hearts: all of this is compressed into this saturating, life-changing tableau of disarmingly simple beauty.

---

[95] "Saturated event" is a term coined by Jean Luc-Marion to describe phenomena that are of such overwhelming givenness or overflowing fulfillment that the intentional acts aimed at these phenomena are overrun, flooded—or 'saturated.' See Marion's work, *In Excess: Studies of Saturated Phenomena.* See also, Christian M. Gschwandtner, *Degrees of Givenness: On Saturation in Jean-Luc Marion.*

"And when they saw it, they understood what had been told them concerning this child."

Here we are reminded of St. John's reaction at the tomb: *"Then the other disciple, who reached the tomb first, also went in, and he saw and believed"* (Jn. 20:8). A moment of recognition. The penny drops, the missing piece of the puzzle appears, the key is discovered that unlocks the entire mystery. For Jesus is, as St. Irenaeus described Him, "the Key Hypothesis."[96] He unlocks the entire meaning of history. He is the Key Piece without which the whole cannot hang together. He is the Missing Term of the world's meaning. He is the Divine *Logos*: the Inner Form of all that is, enabling all that exists to come together in Him. Christ Jesus is *"the cornerstone, in whom the whole structure is joined together and grows into a holy temple in the Lord"* (Eph. 2:20–21). In Him "we live and move and have our being" (Acts 17:28). He is "before all else that is" and in Him all things "are held together" (Col. 1:17). Once He appears, everything becomes clear. Without Him, nothing nothing is properly understood. Without Him, history has no meaning, no purpose, no direction. Without Him, time and space are but a random sequence of events, a cacophony of "sound and fury, signifying nothing."[97]

Consider the following sequence of numbers; "...2...4...?" What is the missing term? What is the formula implied? Until the next, magic number appears, the meaning of the whole is entirely unknown. The sense of the sequence is both unknown and unknowable.

---

[96] *Against the Heresies,* I.10.3. For a full treatment of how Origen, Sts. Ignatius of Antioch, Irenaeus, Didymus, Justin Martyr, Athanasius, Hilary of Poitiers and other patristic interpreters made use of the same idea, see John J. O'Keefe and R. R. Reno, *Sanctified Vision: An Introduction to Early Christian Interpretation of the Bible,* esp. 22-68.

[97] As King Lear says, "To-morrow, and to-morrow, and to-morrow, creeps in this petty pace from day to day, To the last syllable of recorded time; And all our yesterdays have lighted fools. The way to dusty death. Out, out, brief candle! Life's but a walking shadow, a poor player, That struts and frets his hour upon the stage, And then is heard no more. It is a tale Told by an idiot, full of sound and fury, Signifying nothing." Wm. Shakespeare, *Macbeth,* Act 5, Scene 5, lines 19-28.

It is a universe of meaning held in abeyance. So too with the world before Jesus. All was in waiting. Waiting for what? For the One who would unlock the meaning (*logos*) of it all. The One whose Presence would make sense of history before and after His appearance. The One whose very Person would be the Key, the Missing Piece, the Cornerstone everyone has been waiting for to bring them together, to hold them together, to help them to make sense of every aspect of their lives. Jesus is the One. He is the Firstborn of all creation (Col. 1:15). He is the Rock of Ages (cf. Ps. 18) and the One "everyone is looking for" (Jn. 7:11; 11:56;). He is the long-awaited Messiah; the King of Kings and the Lord of lords (1 Tim. 6:15; Rev. 17:14; 19:16). He is the Divine *Logos*, whose appearance in history, as a part of history, is also the Meaning of history. He is the One who imparts life and meaning to every creature in heaven and on earth.

Though long-awaited and much expected, no one expected the Messiah to appear as He did. No one anticipated the advent of the Almighty God as an infant child. The Savior of Israel was expected to appear as the Son of Man envisioned by Daniel: *"And to him was given dominion and glory and kingdom, that all peoples, nations, and languages should serve him; his dominion is an everlasting dominion, which shall not pass away, and his kingdom one that shall not be destroyed"* (Dan. 7:14). Power and might would be His strength, glory and majesty His raiment. Instead what the shepherds behold is a baby borns poverty, weakness, innocence, and vulnerability. They see the Mystery of Divine Relinquishment (*Kenosis*) incarnate before them. The see the Creator of the universe nursing helplessly at His mother's breast. They see the King of heaven lying at their feet.

If nonplussed, the shepherds do not show it. Instead they register a kind of preternatural recognition. Marginalized themselves by a reputation (not undeserved) as thieves and marauders, they somehow experience Jesus as the one who "came to call sinners" (Mk. 2:17; Mt. 9:13). The Lord is already showing Himself to be a light for those sitting in darkness (Isa. 9:2; Mt. 4:16; Jn. 8:12; 12:46). He is already setting the captives free and bringing joy to the downtrodden (Ps. 147:6; Lk. 4:18; Jn. 16:12). Only the pure in spirit can see God (Mt. 5:8). Despite their failings and sins, the shepherds recognize Jesus as the Redeemer, and in this moment of "understanding," they are saved.

Presentation

Luke 2:22

"And when the time came for their purification according to the law of Moses, they brought him up to Jerusalem to present him to the Lord."

The Law of Israel is all about purification. It is all about removing the barriers to perfect union with God. It is about remaining in right relationship with God. "Right relationship" with God is the biblical definition of "righteousness." It is also the underlying meaning of "justification." "Justification" means "being in proper alignment" with God. The Law is God's gift to His chosen people that they might remain in "right relationship" with Him. It enables them to be in a position such that God's glory might be continuously flowing through them. For Israel is chosen and shaped by God so that they might to be "a light unto the nations" (Isa. 2:2-4; 42:1-9; 49:1-6; 56:3-8; 66:18-23; cf. Gen. 12:1-3; Lev. 17:8-9; 22:17-25; 1 Kg. 8:41-24; 2 Chron. 6:32-33). Their purpose is to function as God's instrument of *universal* restoration. Through Israel, God intends to return the world to its Original Unity. Through His Chosen People He desires to reverse the betrayal of Adam and Eve, to redeem the murder of Abel by Cain, and to undo the effects of the Tower of Babel. Through Israel and its Law, God desires to recreate the universe, according to His Original Plan.

The purification desired by all Israelites "zealous for the Law" (Jdth. 9:4; 1 Kg. 19:10-14; 1 Mac. 2:26) was prefigured in the theophany of the Burning Bush (Ex. 3:1-6). There Moses beholds, by way of preview, what God desires for Israel and the world: to glorify all according to His own Divine *Kabod* (Glory). Just as the Burning Bush is incandescent with the Fire of God's Presence - enveloped by Divine

Glory but not destroyed by it - so will Israel, through its devotion to God's Law, be made radiant with love of God. This love of God, in turn, will flow over onto Israel's neighbors, enveloping them with the same consumptive, incandescent love for Yahweh that Israel has. The purpose of the Law is love. "You shall love the Lord your God with all your heart, and with all your soul, and with all your mind. This is the great and first commandment. And a second is like it, You shall love your neighbor as yourself. On these two commandments," Jesus tells us, "depend all the law and the prophets" (Deut. 6:5; Matt. 22:37–40). This is also why Jesus says, "Think not that I have come to abolish the law and the prophets; I have come not to abolish them but to fulfill them" (Matt. 5:17). Understood properly, the Law of Israel is a Divine Gift for His chosen people that they might be unto the world both a magnet and a manifestation of His all-enveloping, all-consuming, all-transfiguring Love.

The Light and Love of the Law, however, are surpassed and replaced in the Person of Jesus. With the advent of the Incarnation, Temple and Torah, Law and Sacrifice are superseded and perfected in the Mystery of the Christ. He renders the Law as superfluous and as obsolete as the does the rising sun the candles used to light the previous night. It is not that the Law is/was not good; rather, "the law [w]as but a shadow of the good things to come instead of the true form of these realities" (Heb. 10:1). Jesus is He whom Law and Burning Bush anticipated. He is the Truth (Jn. 14:6) that issued the Law to begin with. He is the Way that those following the Law have been looking for (Jn. 14:6). He is the Life foreshadowed in the lives of those who kept the Law zealously (Jn. 14:6). Everything prior to Jesus, though essential to the *Economia* of God's Plan, "are only a shadow of what is to come… the substance belongs to Christ." (Col. 2:17). The good is often the enemy of the best, and, in the case of Israel's Law, the purifications recommended by Moses cannot hold a candle to the redemption offered us in Christ.

"...the couple brought Him to Jerusalem..."

We are reminded at once of Palm Sunday. Here Jesus "enters Jerusalem" accompanied by the adoring throng: *"And the crowds that went before him and followed him shouted, "Hosanna to the Son of David! Blessed is he who comes in the name of the Lord! Hosanna in the highest!""* (Matt. 21:9). God's Treasure enters God's City, the city of David. David is God's favored one. To David was it promised, *"When your days are fulfilled and you lie down with your fathers, I will raise up your offspring after you, who shall come forth from your body, and I will establish his kingdom. He shall build a house for my name, and I will establish the throne of his kingdom for ever"* (2 Sam. 7:12–13). *Jesus* is the descendent David was promised. *Jesus* is the offspring of the house of David whose kingdom and throne shall be established forever. His Kingdom, however, shall belong only to the "poor in spirit" (Mt. 5:3). His throne will be that of a Cross. His crown will be one of thorns. His raiment will be the stripes and bruises He bore on account of the sins of those who reject Him (Isa. 53:5; cf. Rom. 4:25; Eph. 2:5).

Jesus will also *"weep over Jerusalem"* because *"you did not know the time of your visitation"* (Lk. 19:41-44). Many who followed Jesus missed their magic moment. They failed to recognize their moment of everlasting opportunity. The riches of the world, the affairs of state, the fear of the future: all of these conspired to prevent many in Israel from discerning the opportunity God was presenting them in Jesus. Following Him was their way to enter the Kingdom of God. They, however, identified entering the Kingdom of God with maintaining the *status quo*. They identified serving God with securing civil and religious peace through ritual and political sacrifice. *Scapegoating* - literally and figuratively - was the foundation of the religious and political order in the city of Jerusalem.

Into this well-oiled machine of sacred, sacrificial violence, Jesus enters as the Lamb of God. He is the baby lamb who will eventually become the city's most famous scapegoat. He is the innocent victim whose murder will be deemed necessary - a sacred duty, as it were - to maintain the peace of Israel. It was Caiaphas who declared, *"it is expedient that one man should die for the people, and that the whole nation should not perish"* (Jn. 11:50). Today, the baby Jesus enters Jerusalem in innocence; later He will be executed just outside the city in ignominy.

"... so He could be presented to the Lord..."

Mary and Joseph freely surrender Jesus into the hands of His Father. They cling to nothing and therefore are free to receive everything from God. What they have received as a gift, they give as a gift (cf. 1 Cor. 4:7). The measure with which they measure out is again measured back to them (Lk. 6:38). In their receiving from God, and then giving to God, and then received again from Him, they participate in an analogous way in the ever-circulating exchange of self-surrendering and ever-receptive love within the Trinity.[98] They are so caught up in the love of God that all they have is both given and received as Gift. Their letting-go of Jesus is pure joy, since their letting-go and receiving-all from Him are simply different sides of their trustful surrender to God.

As good Jews, Joseph and Mary remember the divine act of deliverance from Egypt in which God spared the first born of the Hebrew children, while slaying the firstborn of the Egyptians. Exodus 13 spells out the requirements for all firstborn sons of Israel to be consecrated to the Lord as a response to the sparing of the lives of the firstborn Israelite males during the Passover event. This directive is further developed in Numbers 18, where the Levites will serve on behalf of the firstborn sons. All of Israel's law is a response of gratitude for the mighty acts of election and salvation of Yahweh. Mary and Joseph stand midstream in this tradition of pious gratitude. Like Abel, they give freely of the first-born of what God has given them (Gen. 4:4). Like Samuel, who was taken "to the house of

---

[98] See above, n. 4.

the Lord at Shiloh" when "the child was young" (1 Sam. 1:24), they present Jesus in the Temple in His infancy. Like John the Baptist, Jesus is presented by His parents to be circumcised on the eighth day after his birth (Lk. 2:21). Yet in all of this, New Wine is being poured into old wineskins (Mk. 2:22). The Temple is being invaded by the One who will replace it. The tradition is being inhabited by the One who will transform it. Jerusalem is being visited by the One who will redeem it.

It is worth noting that this ritual of offering one's firstborn son to the Lord in the Temple and then ransoming him back by paying "five shekels of silver" (Num. 18:16), is a merciful rite of redemption that replaces the ancient practice of child sacrifice prevalent throughout all of the ancient Near East, including Israel. It is in Israel alone, however, that the practice of human sacrifice - indeed, of sacrifice in general as the way of ensuring right relation with God and peace and order in society - is *subverted and re-invented*. In Genesis 22 we find the first evidence of of God *replacing human sacrifices with animal sacrifices*. By the end of the prophetic movement in Israel, this tradition will abhor even animal sacrifices, exclaiming with Hosea, Isaiah, Jeremiah, and others, "I desire mercy, not sacrifice." Instead, "the sacrifice acceptable to God is a broken spirit; a broken and contrite heart, O God, thou wilt not despise" (Hos. 6:6; Ps. 51:17; see also: Isa. 1:11-17; 58:5-10; Amos 5:21-24; Mic. 6:6-8; Mt. 9:13; 12:7). Gradually, Israel is distancing itself from the practice of sacred violence. René Girard has called the Hebrew Scriptures a "text in travail."[99] It reveals the Mercy of God, coming to perfection in

---

[99] By this Girard meant that "[T]hroughout the Old Testament, a work of exegesis is in progress, operating precisely the opposite direction to the usual dynamics of mythology and culture. And yet it is impossible to say that this work is complete... sacrifices are criticized, but they continue; the law is simplified and declared to be identical to the love of one's neighbor but it continues. And even though he is presented in a less and less violent form, and becomes more and more benevolent, Yahweh is still the god to whom vengeance belongs. The notion of divine retribution is still alive." (Things Hidden Since the Foundation of the World, 157-158.) It is only

Christ, proleptically purifying God's chosen people of its propensity to scapegoat either animals or people to establish peace. Only Jesus will fully reveal to Israel its habit, like all other peoples, of *"killing the prophets and stoning those who are sent to you!"* (Matt. 23:37).

Jesus comes, then, to gather, not to sacrifice; to envelop, not to exclude or condemn (Jn. 3:17). *"O Jerusalem…How often would I have gathered your children together as a hen gathers her brood under her wings, and you would not!"* (Matt. 23:37). Jesus is the Great Recapitulator, the Great Restorer. He gathers up and recreates all things in Himself. In Him the fullness of God was pleased to reside (Col. 1:19). As God, He comes into the world to bind up the wounds of sinners. He comes to save those who would destroy themselves with sacrificial violence. He does all He can to care for them and to carry them to the Inn of His Father (Lk. 10:34). Jesus is the Divine Physician, the All-Holy Good Samaritan. He is all about healing. His very Name - Jesus ("He who saves") - carries within it the Holy Anointing, the Divine *Salve*, that restores to health what human violence destroys.

Jesus is presented in the Temple as the little child who will one day destroy the Temple (Jn. 2:20; cf. Mk. 14:58). That is to say, He will overturn, not just the money-changers and pigeon sellers, but the entire sacrificial system upon which Israelite religion is established. He will replace the Temple with Himself. He will serve as the *Sacrifice of self-surrender* that will save the human race from needing to sacrifice others in its futile attempts at self-preservation.

"The hour is coming, Jesus tells the Woman at the Well, *"and now is, when the true worshipers will worship the Father in spirit and truth, for such the Father seeks to worship him"* (Jn. 4:23). It is such worshippers as these that Jesus will gather to Himself as He seeks to re-invent Israelite religion to better reflect the non-sacrificial, infinitely gracious nature of His Father. Christianity will be "life in Christ,"

---

with the coming of Christ, Girard insists, that the 'scapegoat mechanism' is revealed for what it is, 'sacred violence' is de-legitimated, and the gospel of unconditional divine non-violent love emerges as the truth about God.

a deeply contemplative and nuptial participation in the Prayer of Jesus. It is never more or less than a complete surrender and joyous self-offering of the Son to the Father. Christian faith is inhabiting the cruciform God.[100] It is entering into the trustful prayer of Jesus on the Cross: *"Father, into thy hands I commit my spirit!"* (Lk. 23:46). It is a real participation in the Sacrifice of Self-Surrender that defines the Person of Jesus Himself. Seeking union with Jesus now replaces all forms of sacred sacrifice that the Temple in Jerusalem both symbolized and sustained.

---

[100] A term coined by Michael J. Gorman in *Inhabiting the Cruciform God: Kenosis, Justification, and Theosis In Paul's Narrative Soteriology.*

"Now there was a man in Jerusalem, whose name was Simeon,
and this man was righteous and devout, looking for the con-
solation of Israel, and the Holy Spirit was upon him."

"Simeon" means "Yahweh has heard."[101] For how many years had
Simeon been consumed by "holy desire"? How long had he desired
to see, to behold the Anointed One of God? Finally, God heard
Simeon's prayer. Indeed, it had been communicated to Him by the
Holy Spirit that he should not die before the dream in his soul should
materialize before his eyes.

This very "holy desire" is itself a great gift of the Holy Spirit. As
St. Paul tells us, *"God is at work in you, both to will and to work for his good*
pleasure." (Phil. 2:13). Simeon is blessed with a holy intuition. He is
afforded a proleptic premonition that the burning desire in his heart
would somehow be fulfilled before his eyes went dark in death. In
this he is a partaker of the same blessing noted by Elizabeth when
the Virgin Mary appeared a her door: *"blessed is she who believed that there*
would be a fulfillment of what was spoken to her from the Lord" (Lk. 1:45).

We are also reminded of St. John of the Cross who wrote:

One dark night,
fired with love's urgent longings
- ah, the sheer grace! -
I went out unseen,
my house being now all stilled
On that glad night,

---

[101] J. L. McKenzie, S.J., *Dictionary of the Bible*, 816.

in secret, for no one saw me,
nor did I look at anything,
with no other light or guide
than the one that burned in my heart.[102]

Simeon is consumed with "love's urgent longings." He is guided into the Temple day after day by "no other light or guide than the one that burned in his heart." Like John of the Cross, Simeon cries out:

Ah, who has the power to heal me?
now wholly surrender yourself!
Do not send me
any more messengers,
they cannot tell me what I must hear.[103]

Simeon desires to see the Messiah face-to-face. He wants to see Him in the flesh. Yet, Simeon also knows not, exactly, what he is looking for. He is not altogether sure what the Redeemer will look like or how He will appear. Like John of the Cross, Simeon confesses his lover's confusion:

All who are free
tell me a thousand graceful things of you;
all wound me more
and leave me dying
of, ah, I-don't-know-what behind their stammering.[104]

So Simeon looks daily for the fulfillment of Malachi's prophecy: *"the Lord whom you seek will suddenly come to his temple; the messenger of the*

---

[102] From his poem, "The Dark Night," stanzas 1, 3.
[103] *Spiritual Canticle*, stanza 6.
[104] Ibid., stanza 7.

covenant in whom you delight, behold, he is coming, says the Lord of hosts." (Mal. 3:1). Simeon's who life revolves around this promise.

We can see in Simeon's trust a recapitulation of the faith of Abraham. Abraham was well over a hundred years old when the promises made to him came to pass (Gen. 12:7-13:15). He kept the flame of faith burning in his heart with 'love's urgent longing' until such time as the word of God spoken to him in secret bore fruit before his eyes (Gen. 18:10). Long before the Book of Revelation was written, both Abraham and Simeon stand as a counter-poise to those of the Church at Ephesus who *'have abandoned the love you had at first."* (Rev. 2:4). Unlike the people of the Church of Sardis, Simeon has not *"grown lukewarm,"* deserving to be *"spewed out of my mouth"* (Rev. 3:16). No, because of his long-suffering faith, Simeon, like Abraham, is "reckoned as righteous" by God and found worthy to have his trust in the Lord's promise to him rewarded (Gen. 15:16; Rom. 4:3-9). In Simeon, as in Abraham and every true disciple of the Lord, we behold *"a true Israelite in whom is no guile!"* (Jn. 1:47).

It is a gift from the Holy Spirit to *"recognize the day of our visitation"* (cf. Lk. 19:44). Just as He does in the Eucharist,[105] the Holy Spirit prepares us to encounter Jesus, makes Him present to us, and unites us to Him in intimate communion. Again, St. John of the Cross beautifully expresses the beauty of this union:

O living flame of love
that tenderly wounds my soul
in its deepest center! Since
now you are not oppressive,
now consummate! if it be your will:
tear through the veil of this sweet encounter![106]

---

[105] CCC 1091-1109.
[106] From his poem, "The Living Flame of Love," stanza 1.

What is the end of the Christian Life? Is it not a participation in the very Life of God Himself? The Mystery of Christ's Incarnation is seamless. The Paschal Mystery is already present in the Presentation. Anagogy is revealed here by way of anticipation. Simeon is anointed by the Holy Spirit that has come down "upon him." The same *Epiclesis* of the Spirit that transubstantiates the bread and wine in liturgy into the Body and Blood of Christ transfigures Simeon into the "I-know-not-what" of his deification in heaven.

Christianity is the on-going Christification of the world through the Spirit of Christ. He descends upon the world in conjunction with the Son's Incarnation and Paschal Mystery. The Spirit that inspired Abraham to move from the land of Ur to the Land promised Him by God, that inspired Simeon to enter the Temple that fateful morning, that inspired Anna to remain forever faithful to the God she worshipped, that inspired Elizabeth to cry out in joy when Mary came to visit, that caused the infant, John, to leap in her womb for joy: this is the same Holy Spirit who imparts the "life to the world" that Jesus came to give (Jn. 6:33). Jesus is the Anointed One. He is anointed with the Holy Spirit who, in turn, anoints the world with the healing Power of God. The goal of the Christian Life is to be made a *pneumatikos* - a Spirit-bearer. It is the Spirit of the Living God who alighted upon Simeon at the Presentation. Simeon it is who affords us an archetypal preview of all those who, in embracing Jesus, will become partakers of His Holy Spirit.

"It was revealed to him by the Holy Spirit that he would not ex-
perience death until he had seen the Anointed of the Lord."

Simeon, though advanced in years, was youthful in hope. He had
reason to get up every morning and go to the Temple. He was on
the lookout for the Promised One of God. Hope is a Gift of the
Holy Spirit, as are knowledge and understanding. These are the
very gifts of discernment and recognition that the Spirit will also
impart to Simeon when Jesus is presented in the Temple. The Spirit
was preparing Simeon for his encounter with Christ long before the
Savior was presented for His Dedication. As we have seen above,
the Spirit of God prepares us to receive the Person of Jesus. Simeon
is fertile ground, prepared to be fecund by the waters of the Holy
Spirit. The Spirit has worked in the mind and heart of Simeon many
decades before he actually encounters Jesus in the Temple. He has
been gradually equipped by the Holy Spirit with an interior vision
and intuition enabling him to recognize the fulfillment of God's
promise to him when the time is ripe.

Simeon's life, therefore, had meaning, and this meaning con-
sisted in looking out for the One St. John described as The Meaning
(*Logos*). "In the beginning was the Meaning (*Logos*). The Meaning
(*Logos*) was with God and the Meaning (*Logos*) was God" (Jn. 1:1).
This is how Pope Benedict XVI translates the opening verse of St.
John's Gospel.[107] Benedict reminds us that *Logos* means "Meaning,"
not simply "Word." Jesus is the Word which, when spoken to the

---

[107] See e.g., Joseph Ratzinger, *Introduction to Christianity*, 26. See also, Benedict XVI,
Dogma and Preaching: Applying Christian Doctrine to Daily Life, 93-95.

world by the Father, furnishes it with its interior, fundamental Meaning. Jesus is the Word/Meaning which, though rejected, has become, for believers, the Cornerstone of the meaning of life. Jesus is the Key *Hypothesis*, as St. Irenaeus tells us,[108] in relation to Whom all other things make sense. No Jesus, no Peace (meaning). Know Jesus, know Peace (Meaning).

Simeon is on familiar terms with the Spirit even prior to the coming of Christ. Like the wind that "blows where it will" (Jn. 3:8), the Spirit is operative even outside His formal Descent on the Feast of Pentecost. "The Spirit had not yet been given" (Jn. 7:39), yet Simeon knew the Holy Spirit quite intimately. How can this be? It is because the immanent Trinity - the Communion of Divine Love that is Father, Son, and Holy Spirit - pre-exists the creation and history of the world. Jesus is the *Eternal* Word. He lives from all eternity *asarkos* (without flesh) in the bosom of the Father prior to becoming e*nsarkos* (enfleshed) through His Incarnation in the womb of Mary. The 'bosom of the Father' includes and makes possible the 'womb of Mary.'

Similarly with the Holy Spirit: He precedes the creation of the world and makes His Presence felt at every point in its genesis. Even when "[t]he earth was without form and void, and darkness was upon the face of the deep; and the Spirit of God was moving over the face of the waters" (Gen. 1:2). The Spirit is ever moving, ever blowing. We notice traces of His Presence, but we "do not know whence it comes or whither it goes" (Jn. 3:8). Father, Son, and Holy Spirit are, each in their own way, infinitely Greater-than any of the dispensational schematics we construct to explain their activity. The Life and Providence of God exceed all sacramental systems and theological theories. As the *Catechism of the Catholic Church* reminds us, "God has bound salvation to the sacrament[s]…but he himself is not

---

[108] See above, n. 96.

bound by his sacraments."[109] God is the Source of the sacramental system, not subject or enslaved to it.

In this we glimpse the 'catholicity' of the Father's love. His love can never be reduced to its cultic expression. The Ever-greater God condescends to establish an Economy of Salvation for our sake but remains Himself unencumbered by it. "God is as Jesus does," most certainly, yet "the Father is greater than I" (Jn. 14:28). The wind of the Father's Spirit blows where it wills. The mysterious operations of Trinitarian Love overflow, exceed, and saturate all the moralistic and sacramental categories that attempt to account for them. Father, Son, and Spirit defy description and they resist systemization. In allowance for our weakness, they furnish us with symbolic expressions of Divine Love that "effect what they signify,"[110] but its purview is cosmic and its magnitude incalculable. "My ways are not your ways," says the Lord (Isa. 55:8). Simeon's familiarity with the Holy Spirit is living proof of the prevenience of God's grace prior to and outside of the frameworks of salvation history and sacramental theology.

It was promised to Simeon that "he would not experience death *until* he had seen the Anointed of the Lord." "*Until*" can have different meanings. Like the word "when," it can mean "up to the time that" or it can mean "never." As in: "You can watch TV until the guests arrive" or "You won't win the lotto until hell freezes over." Scripture tells us that "until the present day" the grave of Moses has not been found (Deut. 34:6). This does not imply that such a discovery is an immanent event. So also with Simeon. Could it be that Luke is telling us here not that Simeon's death is immanent but that his coming encounter with the Lord will transport him directly into eternal life?

"I am the resurrection and the life," Jesus told Mary, "he who believes in me, though he die, yet shall he live, and whoever lives and believes in me shall never die" (Jn 11:25–26). And again, "Truly,

---

[109] CCC 1257.
[110] CCC 1084, 1127.

truly, I say to you, he who hears my word and believes him who sent me, has eternal life; he does not come into judgment, but has passed from death to life" (Jn 5:24). Perhaps what is happening here is not that Simeon's death is being predicted but instead he is being promised what Jesus later proclaimed: to encounter God's Anointed One in Jesus is to pass from death to life in a way that enables the believer to live as though death were not.

Jesus is "the Anointed of the Lord." And, as such, He comes to "anoint the world" with the Abundance of Life He brings from His Father (cf. Jn. 6:33; 10:10). This Life is "the light of the human race" (Jn. 1:3). It is also the Life of His Holy Spirit. Jesus is anointed with the Holy Spirit. The mission of the Spirit is to promote and extend the ministry of the Son (16:13-15), and the mission of the Son is to send the Spirit into the world (Jn. 15:26; 16:7). All the words and actions of Jesus are inspired and guided by the Spirit. The Spirit communicates to the Son what the Father desires (cf. Jn. 15:14). Jesus is a walking theophany of Trinitarian love. "In Him all the fullness of God was pleased to dwell" (Col. 1:19). To encounter Jesus is to enter into eternal life. It is to already "pass from death to life" (Jn. 5:24) and to be set free from our "slavery to the fear of death" (Heb. 2:15).

Surely this was the pre-natal experience of John the Baptist who "leaped for joy" the moment Mary's voice reached the ears of Elizabeth (Lk. 1:44). The arrival of Jesus into the world renders the Law as irrelevant as candlelight to the rising sun. He is the Light of the world (Jn. 8:12; 9:5) making all other lights seem darkness by contrast. In His light we see light (Ps. 36:9). Illumined by his Light and ignited by the fire of His divine Mercy, our faith merges into His fidelity to His Father, making us participants in His "faithfulness unto death." It is the "faithfulness of Jesus Christ" (*pistis Christou*) that is the salvation of the world, and it is *our participation in His fidelity* that constitutes our righteousness, our justification, and our salvation in the eyes of his Father.[111]

Jesus is the "Anointed One," the "*Messiah*" (חָשִׁיחַ *mashiach*, Hebrew) and "*Christ*" (Χριστός *Christos*, Greek) of the Lord. He is the "Holy One of God" whom even the demons call by name (cf. Lk. 4:34). He is saturated by the Spirit from above (cf. Lk. 3:22). Jesus is also the One prefigured in the holy anointings poured out upon priests, prophets and kings in the Old Dispensation (1 Sam. 10:1; 16:13; 2 Kg. 9:6;). He is the one imaged forth in the "oil of gladness" that drips from the beard of Aaron onto the collar of his beautiful robes (Ps. 133:2). He is the One anointed with precious spikenard in anticipation of his death (Mk. 14:8) and anointed after his death with the sacred ointments of aloes and myrrh (cf. Lk. 24:1). He is the Great High Priest anointing us with a share in His own self-surrender to the Father (cf. Heb. 4:16). He is the incarnation of Divine Mercy, anointing us with the aromatic fragrances of love (Mk. 14:3).

The anointing that flows from the Person of Jesus is the opposite of the flow of blood by the woman afflicted with a hemorrhage (Mk. 8:43). Jesus is the Antidote to all that ails us as humans. He exudes the oil of the Holy Spirit. He unleashes a torrent of blood and water

---

[111] The ultimate meaning of the key biblical terms "righteousness," "justification" and "salvation" is "participation in the *pistis Christou*, i.e., in 'the faithfulness of Jesus Christ.'" Adopting a "participative" approach to our Life "in Christ," as well as contemplating the "faithfulness of Christ" vis-a-vis His Father, are key to understanding salvation as *theosis*, i.e., as deification, becoming 'partakers of the divine nature' (2 Pt. 1:4). Scholars developing what is known as the New Perspective on St. Paul have noted that several key passages in St. Paul's writings (notably, Rom. 3:21-26, Gal. 2:15-20; 3:22; Eph. 3:7-12; Phil. 3:89) which say that salvation/justification/righteousness come "through faith *in* Jesus Christ," can also be translated as "through the faith [or faithfulness] *of* Jesus Christ." Translating the preposition as a subjective genitive changes its meaning entirely. It shows that it is *the faith or fidelity of Jesus in His Father's faithfulness that is Mystery of salvation*, and that our righteousness, justification, and salvation involves an *anagogical participation in the fidelity of Jesus*. For an extended discussion of this "participative perspective" on salvation, as well as St. Paul's understanding of the "faithfulness *of* Jesus Christ" (*pistis Christou*), see N. T. Wright, *Pauline Perspectives: Essays on Paul, 1978–2013*, 292-533.

from His crucified body that cleanses and replaces the impurities that afflict those who stand beneath His Cross. The covering in His blood that constitutes our salvation has nothing in common with the sacrificial smearing and sprinkling of blood initiated by Moses (Lev. 8:15ff.). Ours is a covering of consolation, a healing balm, a chrismation of comfort. Jesus anoints us with the Gift of His own Holy Spirit, in whom we are immersed for our christification and pneumatization. Through our anointing with the Holy Spirit we become *pneumatakoi* (Spirit-bearers). We become fruit-bearing branches of the Life-giving Vine.

Luke 2:27-28

"He came to the temple now, inspired by the Holy Spirit, and when the parents brought in the Child Jesus, he took Him in his arms and blessed God."

Simeon is driven into the temple, much as Jesus was driven into the desert following His baptism in the Jordan (Mk. 1:12). The Spirit compels him to do so. He is anticipating he-knows-not what. Isn't this just how the Holy Spirit acts? "Sharper than any two-edged sword," He "pierces to the division of soul and spirit, of joints and marrow, discerning the thoughts and intentions of the heart" (Heb. 4:12). He acts in our intuition long before He directs our behavior. Simeon senses the promptings of the Spirit. He hesitates not a second. He enters the Temple, sensing that he is about to discover "something greater than the temple here" (cf. Mt. 12:42).

The Lord whom Simeon seeks cannot be contained by Temple or Torah. At some level, Simeon must already be aware of this important truth. It accounts for the restlessness and undefined agitation that exists in all the Old Testament prophets and saints. The restlessness of David, for example, made him anxious to do a mighty work for God. Building a temple was David's idea. And, on the surface, it seems a perfectly reasonable and laudable thing to do. After all, David had much to be grateful to God for. Yet, his noble and seemingly sincere intentions are met with a rebuke from God delivered through the prophet, Nathan:

"Go and tell my servant David, 'Thus says the Lord: Would you build me a house to dwell in? I have not dwelt in a house since the day I brought up the sons of Israel from Egypt to this day, but I have been moving about in a tent

for my dwelling. In all places where I have moved with all the sons of Israel, did I speak a word with any of the judges of Israel, whom I commanded to shepherd my people Israel, saying, "Why have you not built me a house of cedar?" ... Thus says the Lord of hosts, I took you from the pasture, from following the sheep, that you should be prince over my people Israel; and I have been with you wherever you went, and have cut off all your enemies from before you; and I will make for you a great name, like the name of the great ones of the earth. And I will appoint a place for my people Israel, and will plant them, that they may dwell in their own place, and be disturbed no more; and violent men shall afflict them no more, as formerly, from the time that I appointed judges over my people Israel; and I will give you rest from all your enemies. Moreover the Lord declares to you that the Lord will make you a house. When your days are fulfilled and you lie down with your fathers, I will raise up your offspring after you, who shall come forth from your body, and I will establish his kingdom. He shall build a house for my name, and I will establish the throne of his kingdom for ever. I will be his father, and he shall be my son. When he commits iniquity, I will chasten him with the rod of men, with the stripes of the sons of men; but I will not take my merciful love from him, as I took it from Saul, whom I put away from before you. And your house and your kingdom shall be made sure for ever before me; your throne shall be established for ever" (2 Sam. 7:5–16).

Salvation is never about what we are doing for God. It is all about what God desires to do in and through us. Nothing is more difficult to grasp than the altogether prevenient initiative of the Trinity in all things human and divine. We look at God through the wrong end of the spiritual telescope when we imagine He is in need of anything we produce. He is completely without needs, save our openness to the Gift He desires to give us, which is none other than the Divine Word of His love. We flourish as a by-product of His Divine Desire. His is an uncontainable love. His is an ineffable goodness diffusive of itself (*bonum diffusive sui*). Perhaps it was St. Irenaeus who best grasped the soteriological prerogative of God when he said so remarkably:

Since he who saves already existed, it was necessary that he who would be saved should come into existence, that the One who saves should not exist in vain.[112]

All is created as a function of *God's need,* as it were, to give expression to His uncontainable love. All comes forth from a love beyond all telling, and all is re-capitulated in that same love in the Mystery of the Incarnation. Creation is the economic expression of an inner-trinitarian explosion of self-expropriating love. Father, Son, and Holy Spirit enjoy a transcendently dynamic exchange that generates a creation whose very fallibility is an occasion for the Savior to exercise His identity as Redeemer.

"...and when the parents brought in the Child Jesus..."

We are struck by the humility of this tableau. Comes now the poor couple from Nazareth, he (Joseph) old enough be her (Mary) grandfather. How unassuming, how strange, they look! Did they look around at the beautiful furnishings of the temple? Did Mary feel at home within its precincts because, as tradition has it, she spent her childhood years in their midst? Was Joseph, the carpenter, awed or overwhelmed by the elegance and of Herod's makeover of Solomon's original edifice? No matter. What strikes us about their appearance in the Temple is its innocent and unremarkable character. Jesus, Mary, and Joseph is the Holy Family whose 'holiness' is altogether hidden.

Observe also Jesus' total dependence on his parents. No one knows Mary is the Immaculate Conception. No one knows Joseph is but the foster-father of Jesus. The only phenomenon that presents itself to us is Jesus' absolute dependence on Joseph and Mary. He places Himself totally in their hands. He does the same when we receive Him in Holy Communion. His defenselessness is arresting.

---

[112] St. Irenaeus, *Against the Heresies,* 3.22.3, quoted in John Behr, *The Mystery of Christ: Life in Death,* 77.

We could spend a lifetime contemplating the weightlessness of Jesus in the Host, and the neediness of the Child Jesus in the arms of his parents. They are the same defining Mystery of the self-effacing Savior.

Hidden most of all is the sacrificial subversion that is transpiring with the appearance of the Lamb of God in the Temple. *Prima facie* Jesus is presented in the Temple in order to "be redeemed" by the sacrifice of "a pair of turtledoves or two young pigeons" (Lk. 2:24). In truth He is there to abolish the religion of sacrificial violence that is the *raison d'être* of the temple. Jesus is the lamb led to the slaughter. Today He is brought to be circumcised by a priest, later He will be brought to be eviscerated on a cross. Here Jesus appears as the ewe of God, as unrecognizable in His infancy as he will be later in His ignominy. Business goes on as usual in the Temple. No one other than Simeon aware that "something greater than the temple is here" (Mt. 12:6).

Is the appearance of Child Jesus in the Temple on this day the fulfillment of the prophecy of Malachi? Is this what the prophet meant when he said, *"the Lord whom you seek will suddenly come to his temple"* (Mal. 3:1)? If so, this is a different kind of theophany than the ones that will follow at Jesus' Baptism in the Jordan (Mt. 3:16-17) or in His Transfiguration on Mt. Tabor (Mk. 9:2-8). But, yes, it *is* a manifestation of His glory. It is an epiphany of His divine greatness. For His greatness and His glory consist in His humility. In His self-effacement, in His *kenosis*, in His self-dispossession. *"Truly, you are a God who hide yourself, O God of Israel, the Savior"* (Isa. 45:15). The glory of Jesus we see manifested in His Transfiguration and elsewhere is but an exteriorization of His interior disposition. His heart is eternally aflame with a love for God and for humankind that forever assumes the form of a servant (Phil. 2:7).

"...he took Him in his arms and blessed God..."

Spontaneously, Simeon grabs for the Child. He takes Jesus in his arms. Did Mary intuit the Spirit flowing through the heart of Simeon, causing him to seek union with her Son? Perhaps. In any event, Simeon has a need to "have and to hold" Jesus "from this day forward." Does Simeon recognize that in doing so he is perhaps acting in a nuptial key? Does he sense that perhaps a divine marriage is about to take place? Clearly his desire to hold Jesus come from a Spirit-inspired desire to somehow become one with Him, to connect with Jesus, to forge a bond, with Him, heart to Heart. Can we discern in Simeon's embrace a confluence of reverence and intimacy, of respect and a desire to ravish and be ravished by the One he holds? No doubt Simeon was slow to give Jesus back to His mother. Later Jesus, aware of the world's need to have Him everywhere and always (cf. Lk. 4:43), would transform Himself into the Eucharistic Lord who could be embraced and consumed by all who share Simeon's inspiration.

The fact that Simeon "took" Jesus in his arms and did not simple "receive" Him from His mother reveals a holy audacity that the Spirit sometimes inspires. Usually we are meant to "receive" Jesus, as we do in Holy Communion. But here Simeon exhibits what the saints have called *parrhesia,* holy boldness. It refers primarily to bold speech but can also include bold actions such as Simeon spontaneously undertakes here. St. Thérèse of Lisieux was known for her *parrhesia,* as was St. Philip Neri, St. Pope John XXIII, and many other saints. Most of all we think of St. Peter whose bold speech received both praise (Mt. 16:17) and rebuke (Mt. 16:23) by Jesus at different times. But always Jesus admired the boldness of Peter's heart, and saw in him one "blessed by my Father" (Mt. 16:17). Jesus' Heart is touched by any person who, inspired by the Holy Spirit, steps out in faith and gives themselves to Jesus (e.g., Mk. 5:34). Sins matter not at all to the Redeemer who looks only for "the one thing needful" (Lk. 10:42), i.e., an openness to the promise of mercy He brings as the Father's beloved Son.

Simenon now spontaneously *"blesses God."* He erupts in an

epiphanic expression of praise. Praise of God is the perfection of the human person. It is culmination and crowing expression of a heart illumined by the Holy Spirit. *"The Spirit himself prays within us with sighs too deep for words,"* St. Paul tells us (Rom. 8:26). He 'lights us up' with His own divine Life, making of us an incandescent instrument of God's Light in the world. The consolation of the Holy Spirit gives both light and heat. Simeon begins to glow with his glorification of God. He is like a thorn bird singing the sweetest song of his life, even as he draws his final breath. In this, perhaps, he prefigures Jesus also, who, Himself impaled on the wood of the cross, utters the exquisitely doleful yet hopeful twenty-second psalm and says with his dying breath, "Father, into your hands I commit my spirit" (Lk. 23:46; cf. Mt. 27:46). In both these expressions of praise we recognize a flaming out that is at once awful and beautiful to behold.

"Now Master, You can dismiss Your servant in
peace; You have fulfilled Your word."

To whom is Simeon speaking? God? Jesus? Does he recognize in the infant his Lord and Master? Is he speaking directly to Jesus, or to the Father? Does he recognize Jesus as a King? Does Simeon connect with Jesus in the same way as the shepherds and the Magi did in the cave in Bethlehem? Jesus is certainly our Master (Mk. 9:5; 10:51; cf. Jn. 13:3). Even Judas acknowledges as much when he addresses Jesus in the Garden, "Hail, Master!" (Mt. 26:49). Is Simeon doing the same when he begins his prayer with *"Now Master..."*?

"You can dismiss Your servant in peace..." We can recognize in Simeon's self-deprecation Jesus' own divine *kenosis. "It is finished,"* says Jesus to His Father on the cross (Jn. 19:30). He, too, is ready to be 'dismissed in peace' now that His mission has been fulfilled. *"No servant is greater than his Master,"* says Jesus (Jn. 13:16). He means this of Himself vis-a-vis His Father, just as Simeon now expresses this same sentiment in his Canticle of Praise.

Simeon is the *"blessed servant whom the master finds vigilant on his arrival..."* (Lk. 12:37). He is also the servant who knows that he is *"an unworthy servant...who has only done what was his duty"* (Lk. 17:10). Yet his vigilance and his humility have now been rewarded. He experiences peace. He has peace that the eternal penny has finally dropped, that the missing piece of the puzzle has finally been discovered. The door of salvation has been unlocked after a lifetime of knocking (Lk. 11:9). Everything now fits together. The world's mosaic has finally found the Cornerstone of its coherence. Jesus has appeared, and Simeon recognizes Him as the One who "makes all things new" (Rev. 21:5). Like Mary in her Immaculate Conception, Simeon, it seems, has received a prevenient share of the grace Jesus pours forth upon the world in His Paschal Mystery. "Peace be with you," he says to his disciples several times upon His Resurrection (Jn. 20:19, 21, 26). "Peace I leave with you, My peace I give you" (Jn. 14:27). Simeon, it seems, even now participates in the eternal life Jesus promises to those who believe (Jn. 5:24; 17:3). Even though he is soon to die, yet is he already living in the light of the risen Lord.

"You have fulfilled your word..."

Simeon gives all the credit to God. Clearly, he is now speaking to God the Father. His words are an exclamation of gratitude. The Father has been true to His promises. Thanks be to God! Like Mary, Simeon is ecstatic that God *"has come to the help of his servant Israel, and has remembered his mercy, as he spoke to our fathers, to Abraham and to his posterity for ever.'"* (Lk. 1:54–55). Abraham, Mary, Simeon: these form a holy, human trinity glorifying the Father for sending His Word into the world. Simeon's faith, like that of Abraham and Mary, has been vindicated. What more is there to live for, Simeon implies, now that the *Logos* (Meaning) has appeared? Simeon has already *"passed from death to life"* (Jn. 5:24). A single glimpse of God-come-in-the-flesh is all he needs to depart this world in peace. The veil between this world and the next has been torn for Simeon (cf. Mt. 27:51; 2 Cor. 3:15-16). And, in thanking the Father for fulfilling His promises, Simeon both glimpses and gives witness to the Trinitarian Mystery making possible the Incarnation.

"For my eyes have seen your salvation which you have pre-
pared in the presence of all peoples."

Seeing is believing, even if *"those are blessed who have not seen and yet believe"* (Jn. 20:29). Simeon sees. He enjoys a kind of sacramental vision. The Mystery is at once revealed and concealed to him in his encounter with Jesus in the arms of His mother. Here he encounters Infinity in an infant, the fulness of God's glory in the child of an adolescent girl. Simeon is bedazzled by this saturating event. It overwhelms his ability to describe it. It is a wonder that Simeon is not rendered as mute as Zachariah was when he encountered the angel in the Holy of Holies (Lk. 1:22).

The 'salvation' Simeon beholds is not a deed but a Person. The whole of redemption reposes in the *Person* of Jesus. His 'work' and His 'Person' are the same. Hence, Jesus can proclaim: *"This is the work of God, that you believe in him whom he has sent.'"* (Jn. 6:29). And, to "believe in" Jesus is never just the equivalent of giving verbal assent (cf. Mk. 7:6; 2 Tim. 3:5). Far from it. Rather, it is to enter into a intimate embrace with the Word-made-flesh that exceeds and overflows all human analogues of being together. Believing "in Jesus" is just that: an inter-penetration of the mind and heart of Jesus, a participation in His body and blood, one that outstrips even Simeon's loving embrace of the beautiful baby presented to him. Believing "in Jesus" is a life-transforming experience deeper than the deepest kiss, more profound, even, than the embryonic union Mary enjoyed with Jesus when He took flesh in her womb. It is an event of divine in-dwelling, an action of deifying 'blending.' It is a mystery of incorporation and co-habitation, inter-penetration and coinherent conjunction. It is the unspeakable *aporia* of God becoming man so man can become God, a mystery that can be glimpsed only in mystically nuptial terms, never in neo-scholastic formulae. Simeon, of course, is fairly ignorant of all of this, save for his illumined intuition. His proclamation of the salvation made manifest in Jesus is anticipatory and proleptic in nature. He enjoys but the faintest foretaste of Christian belief, yet even this is enough to transport him to heaven.

Simeon's revelation is not for him alone. Salvation is on display *"for all the peoples to see."* This Child is given for the healing of the nations (cf. Rev. 2:22). Jesus is no one's private possession. He is public property, raised up on the Cross for "all to see." Pope Benedict XVI once wrote a book called, "Behold the Pierced One."[113] It reminds us of God saying to Satan, "Behold my servant, Job" (Job 1:8), or the reference to Jesus in the words of the prophet Isaiah, *"Behold my servant, whom I uphold, my chosen, in whom my soul delights; I have put my Spirit upon him, he will bring forth justice to the nations."* (Isa. 42:1). Jesus is presented to the world as the Object of its adoration. His very Presence brings healing.

It is the Face of Jesus we behold in the icon of the Sinai *Pantokrator*, the 6th century depiction of the Lord currently adorning a chapel in the Monastery of St. Catherine at the foot of Mt. Sinai. Gazing upon this icon we discover Jesus gazing down upon us. In His eyes we experience what philosophers call "inverse intentionality": we realize that we are seen before we see.[114] Our sense of control is disarmed by the prevenient gaze of the Other. Descartes' *Cogito, ergo sum* ("I think, therefore I am") is replaced by "You look upon me, therefore I am." Or better yet: "You smile upon me, and I come alive!"

Let us behold ourselves in the loving gaze of the Lord. Jesus is the mirror in which we see ourselves. He is the Other who envelops

---

[113] Joseph Ratzinger, *Behold The Pierced One: An Approach to a Spiritual Christology*.
[114] John Panteleimon Manoussakis, *God After Metaphysics: A Theological Aesthetic*, 20ff. See also Jean-Luc Marion, *God Without Being*, 7-24.

us in His love. *"All nations shall come and worship you, for your judgments have been revealed"* (Rev. 15:4). *"They shall look on him whom they have pierced"* (Jn. 19:37). *" Father, I desire that they also, whom you have given me, may be with me where I am, to behold my glory which you have given me in your love for me before the foundation of the world"* (Jn. 17:24). These are some of the promises in the process of being fulfilled when the Child Jesus is presented to Simeon in the Temple.

"Simeon blessed them and said to Mary His Mother, 'This child is destined to be the downfall and rise of many in Israel, a sign that will be opposed.'"

"Simenon blessed them..." One blessed moment; the calm before the storm; a keepsake moment; a moment of blessed recognition. A father expressing a final word of love before going off to war...

We can also hear in Simeon's blessing an echo of the Adoration of the Magi. Or the incredulous words of John the Baptist when asked by Jesus to baptize Him in the River Jordan (Mt. 3:4). It is they who should be blessing Simeon. Instead the Holy Family is blessed by the prophet. The holy man Simeon recognizes "there is something greater than the Temple here" (Mt. 12:6) and so he blesses Mary, Joseph and Jesus.

"He said to Mary His Mother, 'This child is destined to be the downfall and rise of many in Israel...'"

It is Jesus' destiny to be a goad against whom many a person will kick (Acts 26:14). He is the *"fortified wall of bronze against whom they will fight... but not prevail..."* (Jer. 15:20). Yet, His power is not that of steel but of water, Living Water (Jn. 4:10). His gentleness is stronger than steel. It penetrates the rockiest of soil, the hardest of hearts (cf. Mk. 3:5). This child comes to give life and give it in abundance (Jn. 10:10) yet as one destined for an ignominious death. His death is not a maudlin affair. It is simply a matter-of-fact. *"He came to his own, and his own received him not"* (John 1:11-12). Jesus downfall is itself the *downfall* of many. His Passion is a stumbling block, an obstacle, a *skandalon* ('scandal') for those who cannot surrender to Jesus. His death attracts and repels us at the same time. *"Blessed is he who finds no skandalon (σκανδαλισθῇ)* [obstacle, hinderance, stumbling block] *in me,"* He tells the disciples of John the Baptist (Lk. 7:23).

Jesus Himself refuses to be 'scandalized' by Peter. That is, He refuses to stumble over the satanically attractive temptation presented by Peter's misunderstanding of His messianic mission. "Get behind me, Satan," He tells Peter, "you are a σκάνδαλον ['scandal,' hinderance, snare, trap, stumbling block] to me" (Mt. 16:23). Jesus, to be sure, stumbles on His way to Calvary, but His is not the 'scandalous' way of stumbling. He does not succumb to an easier, softer way of salvation. Instead, He moves forward in His totally defenseless self-surrender to the powers of evil (violence). His *kenosis* is our *theosis*. Only through his fearless surrender to the forces of death are we set free from the sin that makes us 'slaves to fear of death' (Heb. 2:15).

Jesus is *"a sign that will be opposed."* In iconography, Mary is often pictured with Jesus in her womb seated on a throne. This icon is called 'Our Lady of the Sign.' Jesus is the Sign, the *Ur-Sakrament*, the fontal Mystery of God. God is as Jesus does. Jesus' Incarnation is that of a Sign. He is the visible manifestation of Trinitarian Love. In Him heaven and earth meet, justice and peace kiss (Ps. 85:11). The finite and the Infinite connect. The world of God and the world of humanity come together in the virginal womb of the Blessed Virgin Mary.

The Sign she carries, however, is rejected by the world. From the very moment of His birth, the 'principalities and powers' governing this world react in apoplectic opposition to the coming of Christ. Herod begins an all-out assault on the infant King. As St. John, the apostle Jesus loved, wrote in his gospel, "He came to His own and His own received Him not" (Jn. 1:11). Judas betrayed Him, Peter denied Him, and His other apostles abandoned Him when He needed them most (Mt. 26:56). The Pharisees, Sadducees, scribes and priests each, in their own way, rejected this Incarnation of the Father's love. Jesus is opposed by friend and foe alike, so foreign in His Life to the life of this world.

"And you yourself shall be pierced with a sword so the
the thoughts of many hearts may be laid bare."

Mary's fate and Jesus' fate are inseparable. All that happens to Him happens also, in a derivative way, to her. Holy Mother and Holy Child remain intimately and emotionally symbiotic even after the umbilical cord is cut. For in His Incarnation, Jesus imparts a share of the inner-Trinitarian inter-connectedness to the human race. He is *never without* His Mother following His conception in her womb just as He is *never without* His Father from all eternity. The same relationship of *mutual inseparability* is established such that everything that happens to Him as Son reverberates profoundly in the heart of His Mother.

Here is how Pope Benedict XVI put it:

> The old man Simeon spoke to you of the sword which would pierce your soul (cf. Lk 2:35), of the sign of contradiction that your Son would be in this world. Then, when Jesus began his public ministry, you had to step aside, so that a new family could grow, the family which it was his mission to establish and which would be made up of those who heard his word and kept it (cf. Lk 11:27f). Notwithstanding the great joy that marked the beginning of Jesus's ministry, in the synagogue of Nazareth you must already have experienced the truth of the saying about the "sign of contradiction" (cf. Lk 4:28ff). In this way you saw the growing power of hostility and rejection which built up around Jesus until the hour of the Cross, when you had to look upon the Savior of the world, the heir of David, the Son of God dying like a failure, exposed to mockery, between criminals. Then you received the word of Jesus: "Woman, behold, your Son!"

(Jn 19:26). From the Cross you received a new mission. From the Cross you became a mother in a new way: the mother of all those who believe in your Son Jesus and wish to follow him. The sword of sorrow pierced your heart. Did hope die? Did the world remain definitively without light, and life without purpose? At that moment, deep down, you probably listened again to the word spoken by the angel in answer to your fear at the time of the Annunciation: "Do not be afraid, Mary!" (Lk 1:30). How many times had the Lord, your Son, said the same thing to his disciples: do not be afraid! In your heart, you heard this word again during the night of Golgotha. Before the hour of his betrayal he had said to his disciples: "Be of good cheer, I have overcome the world" (Jn 16:33). "Let not your hearts be troubled, neither let them be afraid" (Jn 14:27). "Do not be afraid, Mary!" In that hour at Nazareth the angel had also said to you: "Of his kingdom there will be no end" (Lk 1:33). Could it have ended before it began? No, at the foot of the Cross, on the strength of Jesus's own word, you became the mother of believers. In this faith, which even in the darkness of Holy Saturday bore the certitude of hope, you made your way towards Easter morning. ...Thus you remain in the midst of the disciples as their Mother, as the Mother of hope. Holy Mary, Mother of God, our Mother, teach us to believe, to hope, to love with you. Show us the way to his Kingdom! Star of the Sea, shine upon us and guide us on our way![115]

Is there any love like a mother's love? She is deeply wounded when her Son is opposed. She hurts when He hurts. Mary is Rachel-writ-large, weeping for her Child (cf. Jer. 31:15). Jesus, the unblemished Lamb led to the slaughter, is the sum and substance of all Holy Innocents in the world. Mary did you know? Did you know, not only that the Babe you held in your arms would be the Savior of the world, but that His unjust death would be the cost of our redemption? And did you blame yourself? For the slaughter of the Holy Innocents? For the victimage that later reigned down upon your Son? How deeply to heart did you take your Son's own suffering? Was your suffering in some sense greater than His, since you

---

[115] *Spes Salvi*, 50.

knew yourself to be the one who delivered Him into our vicious and violent hands?

Simeon's words are already piercing her soul: "...He will be opposed..." Doubtless this sent a wave of shock through Mary's heart. Were Simeon's words a harbinger of other words that would later wound her soul, for example, "Who are my brothers, who is my mother" (Mt. 12:48) and "...Behold your mother, behold your son" (Jn. 19:26)? But Mary would also hear Jesus say, "Be not afraid" (Lk. 12:32) and "Be of good cheer, I have overcome the world" (Jn. 16:33). As the model of obedience, she would embrace these commands as well, thus experiencing the consolation that attends all who "listen to Him" (cf. Jn. 2:5).

Mary's inseparability from Jesus supplies the motivation for those who would promote her devotion as Co-redemptrix. Perhaps a more mystical view is to see the holy symbiosis of Mother and Son as an extension in time and space of the inseparability between Father and Son. Jesus is as inseparable from the human race in Mary as He is from the heavenly Father in the world of the Spirit. In Mary, Jesus identifies with humanity. When Jesus suffers, Mary suffers. When one suffers, everyone suffers. The Mystical Body of Christ - Head and members in undivided, unconfused union - is firmly established in the womb of Mary.

"When the pair had fulfilled all the prescriptions of the law of the Lord, they returned to Galilee and their own town of Nazareth."

We are struck by the humility of Mary and Joseph returning to Nazareth. Nothing spectacular or special attends their journey. Two poor Jews, returning from whence they came, having done their duty by the law of the Lord. But appearances are deceiving. No doubt Mary and Joseph experienced a certain satisfaction having fulfilled all the requirements of the law. But did they not also experience a growing awareness that, in the Person of their Son, "something greater than the Temple is here" (Mt. 12:6)? Was there perhaps an element of restlessness now present in their practice of the Law? Could they already begin to sense that Jesus would overturn the practices and prejudices of the scribes and priests in Jerusalem?

Recall how St. Paul was torn from the Law during his journey to Damascus, literally knocked off his horse by the blinding Light of the risen Christ (Mt. 9:1-19). As the Light of the world, Jesus reveals the Law to be candlelight - a light shown to be incidental and pre-paratory now that the True Light has appeared. Did the same thing happen with Mary and Joseph? Are they also now being weaned from their own, unquestioned devotion to the Law? Will they soon find fulfilling the law increasingly unsatisfying, knowing they are carrying the Law-giver's Son?

We can imagine devotional priorities of Joseph and Mary shifting. We can see them realizing more and more that the One who "fulfills all righteousness" (Mt. 3:15) is in their care. Being back in Nazareth with Jesus must feel to them like their true coming home to God. Nazareth becomes the New Jerusalem for Mary and Joseph. " I saw no temple in the city, for its temple is the Lord God almighty and the Lamb. The city had no need of sun or moon to shine on it, for the glory of God gave it light, and its lamp was the Lamb" (Rev. 21:22–23).

What a joyous homecoming it must have been for them! They now have Jesus all for themselves! How many years ahead would Mary enjoy before her heart would be pierced by the sword? How many days, months or years would Joseph have to teach his craft to the One he knows to be his own Maker's Son?

"The Child grew in size and strength, filled with wisdom, and the grace of God was upon Him."

Behold the mystery of Jesus' growing! With every passing minute of His life, the Divine Child of God hallows the various developmental dimensions of human living. The stages of Jesus' life are divinized, as it were, as He, the Eternal Word, passes through them. He sanctifies the sequential phases of human persons coming fully to life.

In this 'admirable exchange' of divinity with humanity, the Incarnation itself is somehow progressively actualized in growth of Jesus as a human being. Not only does Jesus' humanity *receive* its divinization by its hypostatic communion with His divinity, but His divine Person also *assumes* all the human dimensions of a child coming to full maturity. "God became man so man could become God,"[116] but God is also progressively 'humanized,' as Jesus 'grew in size and strength' (cf. Lk. 2:40). Yes, the fulness of a Divine Person inhabits the body and soul of this little boy in Nazareth. The Eternal Word remains unchanged in him as the Child grows. Yet, the Divine Word also acquires, in a manner as progressive as the Child's human growth, the mental, emotional, and affective characteristics that develop in the boy's expanding *soma* and *psyche*. The "divine-humanity" of the Incarnate Word is realized and matures during the course of Christ's earthly life. Jesus doesn't become 'more God' as He grows up in Nazareth; but, God, it seems, takes on a more intimate coinherence with human nature as the Redeemer 'grows in size and strength.'

---

[116] See above, n. 48.

The Divine-Humanity of Jesus, the heavenly God-Man, implies a certain pan*en*theism that makes us uncomfortable. Not only does God become man in Jesus, but men and women also become God through this same admirable exchange. The thought of God including us as necessary and contributive members of His own trinitarian Life seems incomprehensible to us. Yet, the identity of God with humanity in the Person of Jesus "signifies not only the divinity of man but also *a certain humanity of God,* [for as Scripture says] 'we are…his offspring (Acts 17:28).'"[117] In and through Jesus humanity participates in the Divine world. It has pleased the Trinity to enable us, in Christ, to contribute to the fulness of the life of Divinity. "God needs the world and it could not have remained uncreated… [for] God is love, and it is proper for love to love and to expand in love. And for divine love it is proper not only to be realized within the confines of Divinity but also to expand beyond these confines. Otherwise, absoluteness itself becomes a limit for the Absolute, a limit of self-love or self-affirmation, and that would attest to the limitedness of the Absolute's omnipotence - to its impotence, as it were, beyond the limits of itself…In the insatiability of His love, which is divinely satiated in Him Himself, in His own life, God goes out of Himself towards creation, in order to love, outside Himself, not-Himself. This extra divine being is precisely the world, or creation."[118] All of this is implied in the simple words, *"he Child grew in size and strength…"*

He was also *"…filled with wisdom…"*

Divine Wisdom is most often associated with the Holy Spirit. Jesus was filled with the Holy Spirit from the moment of His conception. Jesus is indeed the Spirit-bearer, the *Christos,* the Anointed One. He is anointed with the Spirit of His Father, as He 'proceeds from the Father.' Jesus is both the *recipient* of the Father's Spirit and the *dispenser* of the Spirit. He *receives* the Holy Spirit at His Baptism

---

[117] Sergius Bulgakov, *The Lamb of God*, 112 (emphasis added).

[118] Ibid., 120.

and He *sends* the Holy Spirit in His Ascension. He 'sends' to His disciples the very Spirit who 'conceives' Him in the womb of Mary (Lk. 1:35) and who 'drives' Him into the desert after His Baptism by John (Mk. 1:12). Jesus is consubstantial with the Spirit, just as He is consubstantial with the Father. The Spirit is 'God from God, Light from Light,' even as Jesus enjoys the same relation with the Father. The different roles of Son and Spirit in the economy of salvation should not blind us to the mystery of their tri-hypostatic unity from all eternity in their inner (immanent) trinitarian relations.

Because of this close association with the Holy Spirit, Scripture describes Divine Wisdom as 'living with God' from the beginning. (Prv. 8:22; cf. Wis. 8:3). She is 'an initiate in the knowledge of God,' and 'an associate in his works' (Wis. 8:4; cf. Prv. 8:30). She is the 'fashioner of all things.' 'She can do all things, while remaining in herself.' She 'renews all things…[and] is more beautiful than the sun.' She 'excels every constellation of the stars.' Compared with the light 'she is found to be superior,' for the light of day is succeeded by the night, but against wisdom 'evil does not prevail.' She reaches 'mightily from one end of the earth to the other,' and she 'orders all things well' (Wis.7:24, 27–8:1).

All of these beautiful descriptives can be predicated of Jesus as well. Jesus is not only "filled with" Divine Wisdom but can actually be identified with it.[119] He lives with God: "In the beginning was the Word, and the Word was with God, and the Word was God" (Jn. 1:1). He is the 'fashioner of all things': "all things were made through him, and without him was not anything made that was made" (Jn. 1:1–3). He renews all things: "Behold, I make all things new" (Rev. 21:5). He is more beautiful than the sun, excelling every constellation and the Uncreated Source of all light: "I am the light of the world; he who follows me will not walk in darkness, but will have the light of life" (Jn. 8:12). "In Your light, O Lord, we see light" (Ps. 36:9).

---

[119] St. Louis de Montfort made this identification of Jesus with Divine Wisdom in his book, *The Love of Eternal Wisdom.*

Against this Light of the world, even the powers of darkness of evil cannot prevail: "The light shines in the darkness, and the darkness has not overcome it" (Jn. 1:5).

The Wisdom of God, therefore, proceeds from the Father through both Jesus and the Holy Spirit. They were there 'with God in the beginning': "...the Spirit of God was moving over the face of the waters" (Gen. 1:2) while it was through the Word of God that "all things were created, in heaven and on earth, visible and invisible, whether thrones or dominions or principalities or authorities—all things were created through him and for him" (Col. 1:16). Jesus and the Holy Spirit are the "two hands of the Father,"[120] working together to carry out the Father's desires, both in creation and in the re-creation known as redemption.

Divine Wisdom is also called the *Hagia Sophia* (Holy Wisdom) of God. Holy *Sophia* is not the 'feminine principle in God,' as some might allege. The Gnostic gospels are mistaken when they imply that Jesus was married to Mary Magdalene. He is wedded instead to Holy Wisdom, the Father's *Hagia Sophia*. If Jesus has a Divine Spouse is the Holy *Sophia*, not the converted woman from *Migdal Nunayah* (Magdala).

The Divine Wisdom of God - the Holy Spirit of God - is "God from God, Light from Light, true God from true God." What is said of Jesus in the Nicene Creed can also be said of the Father's Holy Spirit. The Holy Spirit is not 'the feminine principle in God,' but the Proto-Image of all things feminine. *Hagia Sophia* is the Divine *Anima*: 'She' who was with God in the beginning, 'the fashioner of all things,' the very Breath of God (cf. Wis. 7:25; 8:1-3). This Divine Wisdom is properly called 'She' because, as the elusive trinitarian Third Person, her defining mission is to both reveal and conceal the indefinable union of the Father and the Son, and to be the Joy of their communion. The Spirit delights, as it were, in the mutual

---

[120] St. Ireneaus, *Against Heresies*, V, 6, 1. Quoted in a different but equally illuminating context by Benedict XVI in *Verbum Domini*, 15.

self-dispossession of Father and Son. "This is My beloved Son, in whom I am well pleased!," says the Father (Mt. 3:17). Holy *Sophia* is She who constitutes the delight the Father takes in the Son and the Son takes in the Father (cf. Jn. 12:28).

Wisdom is also *Sapientia.* Jesus is filled with divine *Sapientia,* saturated with it. *Sapientia* seems a kind of 'oil of unctuousness.' Jesus is shot through with this sapiential anointing. He glistens with the oil of salvation. Like the oil flowing down upon the beard of Aaron (Ps. 133:2) but richer and more internal, the Father's divine *Sapientia* permeates Jesus. It is a soothing, healing, enriching chrism that emanates from His eyes, His words, and His hands. The Spirit of God 'pours forth' from the Lord. His every look, every gesture, every utterance is filled with Holy Wisdom. It is lavishly imparted to everyone who opens to Him.

"...and the grace of God was upon Him...

This phrase recalls the mystery of Holy *Sophia.* The *Anima* of God is both God and not God. Holy *Sophia* was "with God from the beginning" (Wis. 6:22; 9:8) and even "searches the deep things of God" (1 Cor. 2:10), but it is not exactly the same thing as God Himself. Like the divine "Energies of God" spoken of by the eastern church fathers, the "grace of God" is "of God" and "from God" but is not exactly identical with God. "Essence and Energies" always remain distinct within God, yet His Energies partake of His Essence and flow into the world as an economic extension of His ineffable Life.[121] The "Grace" of God, like the "Wisdom" or *Sophia* of God,

---

[121] For a discussion of the difference between God's Essence and His Energies from an eastern Orthodox position, see the chapter, "Essence and Energies" in Vladimir Lossky, *In the Image and Likeness of God*, 176-178. A Catholic version of the same sensibility can be glimpsed here in this beautiful description of Jesus healing of the leper found in the commentary by Erasmo Leiva-Merikakas, *Fire of Mercy, Heart of the Word: Meditations on the Gospel According to Saint Matthew*, volume 1, 325: "All the world's millennial expectation of new and lasting life converges with powerful magnetism

is a certain emanating communication of Divine Life coming forth from God. It is "of God" and redounds with deifying effect to the benefit of the recipient. In the case of Jesus - Himself already divine and in no need of deification as the Father's Only-begotten Son - we can imagine the "grace of God upon Him." Such grace is the "Delight" the Father takes in Jesus. The Father delights to give all He is and has to His Son. The Father is similarly delighted to see how completely His Son receives everything He has to give Him (Mt. 11:27; Jn. 3:35). Finally the Father delights in how perfectly the Son reflects His (the Father's) total self-dispossession through His (the Son's) own self-emptying in the drama of our salvation. All of this is perfectly summed up when the Father is heard to say, "This is my beloved Son with whom I am well pleased!" (Mt. 3:17; cf. 17:5).

---

in that transcendental moment when *the divine energy passes from God through Jesus* into the dissolving flesh of the leper [emphasis added].

Finding

Luke 2:42

"And when He was twelve they went up for the celebration as was their custom."

Jesus is the driver of the action. He is the central Actor in history, just as He is the central Actor in the Eucharist. Both time and space cohere in the *Logos* of God. Nothing happens but that it has an intrinsic relation with Him. *"For in him all things were created, in heaven and on earth, visible and invisible, whether thrones or dominions or principalities or authorities—all things were created through him and for him."* (Col. 1:16). He is the *Logos* of the *logoi*: the Eternal Word furnishing the coherence and meaning to all created things. Now, at the liminal age of twelve, Jesus is on the move. Like the sun in the sky, He, the true Son of God, *"comes forth like a bridegroom leaving his chamber, and like a strong man"* begins to *"run His course with joy"* (Ps. 19:5).

Twelve, as we know, represents a certain fulness: twelve tribes of Israel, twelve apostles, twelve months in a year. It is the fulness of time that seems intended here. *"In the fulness of time God sent forth His Son"* to be our Savior (Gal. 4:4). It is now Jesus' time to act. It is Jesus' time to begin to manifest His glory. God's time is always *kairos* (timeliness) before it is *chronos* (chronology). Better put: history is driven by the providential timing of God. *Chronos* depends on the *kairos* of the *Logos*. Now the *Logos* is in motion. The time has come for Him to continue His revelation of *"the mystery hidden for ages and generations but now made manifest to his saints"* (Col. 1:26).

"…they went up for the celebration as was their custom…"

"Celebration" connotes something vibrant, something fresh, something new. "Custom" designates something contained, something staid, something safe. Doubtless Jesus is now comfortable in the "containers" of Israelite religion. He has learned the commandments, He has acquired the customs of His ancestors, He is familiar with the Temple, He has been going there now for some years with His parents. But this year is different. A new aeon is dawning. Something altogether different, something altogether more vibrant is fermenting. Not only is Jesus becoming, technically, a man; He is now prepared to make known that He is something more than a man. Jesus is the New Wine. The Temple and all it represents are the old wineskins. The wineskins are about to burst. Yet, as Jesus and his parents go *"up for the celebration as was their custom,"* there appears to be *"nothing new under the sun"* (Eccl. 1:9).

> *"As they were returning at the end of the feast, the Child*
> *Jesus remained behind unknown to His parents."*

Those who have attended the feast now return to their ordinary routine. Business as usual re-commences. But not for Jesus. He *"remained behind."* Those who have attended the celebration are unaware of the interior depths of time. They do not know that with the coming of Jesus, *chronos* has been impregnated with *kairos*. Jesus' time has come. His 'Hour' has begun (cf. Jn. 2:4). A kind of universal Daylight Savings Time has been established, such that all historical time, regardless of time zone, has been redeemed by the Daylight from on high. A New Time has begun. A New Day has dawned. Yet, no one is aware of this fact other than the Child Jesus Himself.

It is *"the end of the feast,"* both figuratively and literally. Jesus is the End of religion. Jesus is the End of the Law. Jesus renders anachronistic and irrelevant all ritualistic attempts to remain in right relationship with God. Jesus replaces all sacrificial systems of sacred security with His offer that we participate with Him in His abandonment to His Father. Participation in the Prayer of Jesus is the replacement of all former and future attempts at ritualistic religion.

Jesus is the Kingdom of God in the flesh. He is the *Autobasileia*: the Absolutely Singular Cornerstone of the Divine Edifice known as the *Totus Christus,* the Total Christ. Jesus has come to "reconcile all things to himself, whether on earth or in heaven, making peace by the blood of his cross" (Col. 1:20). Jesus renders the feasts of Israel irrelevant when compared to the "something greater than the Temple here" (Mt. 12:6). Jesus is the End of cultic religion, even if the Mystery of His risen Presence continues to be mediated in cultic form.

"The Child Jesus remained behind…"

The Father's house functions like a magnet for Jesus. He is in-eluctably drawn there. He loves the Law His Father has given. He is attracted to all who attend to the Law and love it as He does. "I have not come to abolish the Law," He will eventually tells His disciples, "but to fulfill it" (Mt. 5:17). Jesus loves the atmosphere of Jerusalem, of the Temple. He loves the *ethos* of adoration. So He *"remains behind"* in the city to follow where the Father is leading Him.

In so doing, Jesus demonstrates total trust. He exhibits the kind of childlike trust He would later so often commend to His followers (Mk. 10:15). He is confident that His Father will provide (cf. Gen. 22:8). He enters the unknown without fear. He enters the dark of that first night in Jerusalem with the light of His Father's Spirit burning in His Heart. Already He is operating according to the promptings of the Holy Spirit. His loyalties transcend His immediate family. It's as if we can already hear Jesus saying, "But who are my mother? Who are my brothers? Are they not the one's who desire to do the will of my Father?" (Mt. 12:48). There is something there for Him yet to do. His business related to the Passover feast is not yet finished. Only many years later will He be able to say about His work in Jerusalem, "It is finished" (Jn. 19:30).

In this *"staying behind"* Jesus seems invisible. He disappears with-out fanfare. He assumes a presence that is totally anonymous, unob-trusive. In this we glimpse his humility, as well as catch a porto-ty-pological flash of His Resurrection. He disappears from his family only to re-appear in the Temple, as if to repeat His sudden appear-ance in the Temple that morning when Simeon recognized the time of his visitation by the Messiah (Lk. 2:27). "…and the Lord whom you seek will suddenly come to his temple…behold, he is coming, says the Lord of hosts." (Mal. 3:1).

All of this is *"unknown to his parents."*

Jesus inhabits a different world from his parents. Their world is enfolded into His, and His world supersedes theirs. They will never fully understand Him. Mary will always only be able to "ponder these things in her heart" (Lk. 1:29; 2:19). For Jesus can be known, as He desires and allows Himself to be known, only by love, not by anything else. "My ways are not your ways, says the Lord" (Isa. 55:8). Here we see the first example of this eternal truth in Jesus' decision to "stay behind" without his parents knowing.

Much of course, *can* be know about the Person of Jesus Christ. His public life is out there, on display, for everyone to see. Yet, the acquisition of the "mind and heart of Christ" (Phil. 2:5; cf. 1 Cor. 2:16) - the goal of our life "in Christ" - is of an altogether different order. Union with Christ - our assimilation into His triune Life - cannot be reached through speculation alone. The light of revelation is uncreated, and as such is darkness to the human intellect. Jesus is revealed to "pure of the heart," especially to hearts purified of the sin of intellectual pride. "God opposes the proud, but gives grace to the humble" (Prv. 3:34; cf. Jas. 4:6; 1 Pt. 5:5;). Intellectual exegesis is relatively fruitless without the grace of contemplation. *Lectio divina* in an anagogical key is the only effective way to approach the Word of God if we really wish to attain to the Living Word contained therein.[122]

---

[122] cf. CCC 108: "…the Christian faith is not a 'religion of the book.' Christianity is the religion of the 'Word' of God, a word which is 'not a written and mute word, but the Word which is incarnate and living.' If the Scriptures are not to remain a dead letter, Christ, the eternal Word of the living God, must, through the Holy Spirit, 'open [our] minds to understand the Scriptures.' (citing St. Bernard, *S. missus est hom.* 4, 11: PL 183, 86 and *Lk* 24:45.) See also my book, *Deified Vision: Towards and Anagogical Catholicism.*

$\mathcal{L}$uke 2:44

"Thinking He was in the party, they continued their journey for a day, looking for Him among their relatives and acquaintances..."

How easy it is to neglect our relationship with Jesus. How easy it is to presume upon His presence with us. Life happens. The business of ordinary existence compels us to 'get on with things.' If even Joseph and Mary can get caught up in the hubbub of everyday living and momentarily lose sight of the Son, how much more so must we be inclined towards inattention in our relationship with the Lord?

Yet, complacency is the great killer of the spiritual life. Benign neglect keeps more good people from ever becoming the saints the Father desires them to become. It is so easy - so natural, so human, yet so deleterious - to take our relationship with Jesus for granted. Even His closest disciples fell asleep when He needed them most. "Could you not watch with me for one hour?," the Lord asks His chief apostle (Mt. 26:40). Would that we were not more like young Samuel, attentive in the watches of the night for the voice of the Lord (1 Sam. 3:1-18).

Often Jesus urges vigilance upon those who would be His disciples. "Stay awake!," He tells them, "for you do not know on which day your Lord will come" (Mt. 24:50). "Be vigilant," He says, and imitate those wise virgins who, yearning for the Bridegroom throughout the night, are found watching and waiting and perfectly prepared upon His return (Mt. 25:1-13). Be like Mary, who, through holy anticipation and humble expectation was perfectly disposed to receive the Word of God when He was announced to her by the angel (Lk. 1:28ff.). Or be like the lover in the Song of Songs who asks repeatedly, "'Have you seen him whom my soul loves?'" (Song 3:3). For even though she slept, her heart "was awake" (Song 5:2). We pray for the grace to remain finely attuned to the Presence of the Lord, developing the vigilance of heart needed to receive the Eternal Word.

We now find Mary and Joseph *"looking for Jesus among their relatives and acquaintances..."* Again, it is natural and easy to look for Jesus in our social relationships. Being surrounded by relatives and friends who share our faith is itself a stimulus to greater faith. Yet, friendship with believers is not the same as intimacy with Christ. Christian community - *koinonia*, fellowship - is never identical with life "in Christ." The Second Great Commandment ("Love your neighbor as yourself" [Lev. 19:18: cf. Mt. 19:19]) cannot replace the First Great Commandment ("Love the Lord your God with all your heart, and with all your soul, and with all your might" [Dt. 6:5; cf. Lk. 10:27]). Nor can the First Great Commandment ever be reduced to the Second. Yes, "where two or three are gathered in my name, there am I in the midst of them" (Mt. 18:20); but, the call of Christ always remains intensely personal, as when Jesus asked His disciples, "who do you say that I am?" (Lk. 9:20), or as "when he looked up and said to [Zacchaeus], "Zacchaeus, make haste and come down; for I must stay at your house today" (Lk. 19:5), or as when he said to Matthew, sitting there at his tax-collecting post, "Follow me!" (Mt. 9:9). The call of Jesus is irreducibly individual. No one but I can answer for myself. All the daughters of Jerusalem cannot tell the lover of Jesus where He can be found (cf. Sg. 6:1). The final truth is: "I am my beloved's, and his desire is for me" (Sg. 7:10). This leaves "looking for Jesus among our relatives and acquaintances" finally unsatisfying in our relationship with Christ.

"Not finding Him, they returned to Jerusalem in search of Him."

Panic. Alarm. Desperation. These and many other such emotions must have transfixed Mary and Joseph when they realized Jesus was not among their company. Already, in their experience of losing Him, Jesus is revealing Himself as "the one thing necessary" (Lk. 10:42). He is the "Pearl of Great Price" (Mt. 13:46), the loss of which is experienced as hell. For did not Mary and Joseph feel like they had fallen into a black hole from which there may be no redemption? That they had lost the Key to Life, the Key to the Kingdom of God? Jesus is greater than life itself. Mary and Joseph are now experiencing this truth as they begin their own kind of "descent into hell." For they are without Jesus and filled with bitter remorse that they may have lost forever the Great Treasure (Mt. 13:44; cf. 6:21) with which they had been entrusted.

Nothing is worse than *"not finding Him."* Misery is being unable to pray, being unable to connect with Jesus. No Jesus, no peace. Know Jesus, know peace. Nothing can substitute for our communion with Christ. And nothing is worse than losing our connection with the One who loves us. Would that the world could realize that the pain of human loss is but a tiny intimation of losing personal contact with God. The loss of a child, for example, is a little taste of hell. An entire life with a close connection with God is a 'chronicle of wasted time.'[123]

---

[123] Malcom Muggeridge retitled his autobiography, *Chronicles of Wasted Time* to connote how vapid his life was before his conversion to Catholicism in his mid-80's, following a life-transforming encounter with St. Theresa of Calcutta.

But even the worst human grief contains within it the affirmation of love. For human grief is the underside of love; the pain of human loss the underside of joy. Grief and and the pain of loss testify to the fact that "His love endures forever" (Ps. 100:5). We wouldn't grieve so much at the loss of a loved one if love itself were not stronger than death (Song. 8:6). The depth of our grief is the measure of our love. And that love cannot be killed. Life is not circumscribed by death, but death by life. "A light has appeared in the darkness and the darkness cannot overcome it" (Jn. 1:5). Good and evil, light and darkness, life and death are not equal opposites. Good is stronger than evil, light conquers the darkness, life circumscribes death.

For those who seek Jesus, desolation can be seen as a gift from God. As those who have recovered from various addictions sometimes say, "When the pain of holding on becomes greater than the pain of letting go, one will let go." Panic can be our friend when it serves as a catalyst for conversion. Our pain can become a gift if it serves as the pre-condition for a new life. In every event, even those involving grief and loss, God is present as love calling us to believe in love. He permits our loss so that we may gain His all.

Mary and Joseph now *"return to Jerusalem in search of Him."*

They don't know where He is, and it is beginning, perhaps, to dawn on them that they also do not exactly know *who* He is. For Jesus always exceeds and confounds our expectations. Every day is a new search for Jesus, every day is a new beginning "in Him." Jesus is a Mystery who is new every day. Like the Magi at Epiphany, and like Mary and Joseph on their way back to Jerusalem, we may 'go in search' of Him, but ultimately we must be led to Jesus by the Holy Spirit. "No one comes to me unless the Father draws him" (Jn. 6:44). It is the Holy Spirit who facilitates the Father's decision to send us in search of Jesus.

Our search for Christ can never presume upon His static presence among us. In His risen life, He is as elusive as when He first appeared to His disciples after His resurrection (Lk. 24:31). The risen Lord, the Eternal Word, the Son of Mary and Joseph: this Jesus is a *Mystery* to be continually re-discovered. Every day we must seek Him as if for the very first time. We are ever-new, ever-young in His presence. This is because He, as our Savior, is Ever-Greater, Ever-New, Ever-More than we can conceive or believe.

All of life is a search for Jesus. He is the *Logos* of our *logoi*. He is the Proto-Image of the Father, and we are "images of the Image."[124] Until I discover Him, I do not know myself. Yet, even in the discovery of Jesus, a radical 'otherness' remains. He is He and I am me. The irreducibility of personal selfhood is enhanced, not eliminated, in my encounter with Christ. This is why we say God remains a Mystery even in the Beatific Vision. I come into my own only when I discover Jesus, but even in this encounter He reveals Himself as the 'Other other.' He also reveals me to myself, not as a clone of Himself but as a mystery as singular as Himself. At the same time, I am forever dependent upon Him for my own personal fulfillment. Our search for Jesus is an insatiable hunger and thirst, the very satisfaction of which is its own ecstatic exacerbation. It begins with our creation by Him and extends through eternity.

---

[124] "When Adam was created in the image and likeness of God, we all were created in him, with a nature capable of being conformed to the Word of God. Therefore Adam, who contains all human nature in himself, and is therefore *'humanity,' is created in the image of the Image of God,* Who has already decided, from all eternity, to become man in Jesus Christ. Hence in his very creation, Adam is a representation of Christ Who is to come. And we too, from the very moment we come into existence, are potential representations of Christ simply because we possess the human nature which was created in Him and was assumed by Him in the Incarnation, saved by Him on the Cross and glorified by Him in His Ascension." Thomas Merton, *The New Man, 94.*

$\mathcal{L}$uke 2:46-47

> *"On the third day they came upon Him in the temple sitting in the midst of the teachers...All who heard Him were amazed at His intelligence and His answers."*

"On the third day they came upon Him..." Jesus appears to His parents in a kind of proto-resurrection event. Thinking Him lost, they discover Him alive. Here Jesus is already revealing Himself as 'the Resurrection and the Life' (Jn. 11:25), not simply as one who will later 'rise from the dead.' For in Him nothing is ever lost. In Him, death itself is circumscribed by Life. In Him is the joy of perpetual discovery. The lost sheep is retrieved (Mt. 10:6; 15:24), the lost coin is found (Lk. 15:9), the lost son is redeemed (Lk. 15:24). In Christ, lostness itself loses its meaning.

Every encounter with Jesus is a glorious epiphany, His every appearance an arresting surprise. Jesus is always there, always ahead of us, always present and risen even when we feel bereft and abandoned. Nothing is ever lost that has been entrusted to the Lord by His Father. "The Father loves the Son, and has given all things into his hand...and this is the will of him who sent me, that I should lose nothing of all that he has given me, but raise it up at the last day" (Jn. 3:35; 6:39).

Many epiphanic events occurred *"on the third day."*

On the third day Abraham beheld the sacred place where he would demonstrate his trust in YHWH by surrendering his son in sacrifice (Gen. 22:4). *On the third day* Moses told the people to *"be ready...for on the third day the Lord will come down upon Mount Sinai in the sight of all the people"* (Ex. 19:11). The prophet Hosea unwittingly foretold the good news of the resurrection when he announced to the people, *"after two days he will revive us; on the third day he will raise us up, that we may live before him"* (Hos. 6:2). In the New Testament, St. John tells us, *"On the third day there was a marriage at Cana in Galilee, and the mother of Jesus was there"* (Jn. 2:1). And how often did Jesus tell his disciples, *"the Son of man must suffer many things, and be rejected by the elders and chief priests and scribes, and be killed, and on the third day be raised"* (Lk. 9:22)? *The third day* is often the occasion for the revelation of the Son's glory in the Scriptures, and his parents' discovery of Jesus in the Temple *"on the third day"* is certainly no coincidence.

In the Temple, we find Jesus *"sitting in the midst of the teachers..."*

Jesus is reposing among the teachers of the Law. He is sitting with *gravitas* in the company of the leading scholars of Israel. Here we recall a similar event later in the life of Jesus when, in the synagogue at Nazareth, Jesus reads from the scroll of Isaiah, *"The Spirit of the Lord is upon me, because he has anointed me to preach good news to the poor. He has sent me to proclaim release to the captives and recovering of sight to the blind, to set at liberty those who are oppressed"* (Lk. 4:18). Rolling up the scroll and handing it back to the attendant, Jesus *"sat down, and the eyes of all in the synagogue were fixed on him"* (Lk 4:20). *Seated there,* Jesus' Presence is magnetic. He holds the gathered believers spellbound. We see Him assuming the same magisterial posture atop the mountain when He calls His apostles (Lk. 6:12). We see Him seated in the boat when teaching the throngs along the shore (Mk. 3:9). We see Him seated at table with His disciples when delivering them - and us - the Gift and Mystery of the Eucharist (Lk. 22:14).

To sit is to repose. To repose is to dwell. To dwell is to abide. To abide is to experience increased intimacy. In sitting amidst the teachers in the Temple, Jesus is manifesting His insatiable desire to intensify His relationship with His Father's chosen people, to gain permanent entrée into the heart of Israel. Jesus comes to call us to communion. How many seated around Him that day comprehended the mystical marriage Jesus desired to effect with them?

He is seated *"in the midst of the teachers..."*

But "you have only one Teacher, the Christ" (Mt. 23:10). Jesus is the *Pantokrator*: the Rule of the Universe and the Incarnation of Divine Wisdom. He is anointed with the Spirit of Wisdom (Wis. 1:6; 7:7, 22; Sir. 15:5; 39:6). Associated with Him, we acquire His divine Wisdom by osmosis. His Wisdom is not something 'obtained' through human effort. Divine *Sapientia* is caught, not taught. As "it is written in the prophets, 'And they shall all be taught by God'" (Jn. 6:45a). Jesus is God, sitting here amidst the teachers of Israel, yet He Himself is the only true Teacher. He gladly imparts to all who "come to Him from the Father" (cf. Jn. 6:45b) the Wisdom of His Holy Spirit.

The humility of Jesus "sitting amidst the teachers" is yet another revelation of His divine *kenosis*. For "though he was in the form of God, Jesus not count equality with God a thing to be grasped" (Phil. 2:6). He allowed Himself to be anointed from above with Divine Wisdom. Relinquishing any claim to divine omniscience, "Jesus increased in wisdom and in stature, and in favor with God and man" (Lk. 2:52). He accepted the ignorance of adolescence to manifest the wisdom of the *Ur-Kenosis*.[125]

"All who heard him were amazed at his intelligence and His answers."

They were more than amazed, they were confounded. Astounded and confounded. Placed precariously on that razor's edge between marveling at Him and wanting to murder Him. Immediately we

---

[125] This is a term favored by Hans Urs von Balthasar and Adrienne von Speyr to connote the self-dispossession and reciprocal self-surrender (self-emptying) that defines the heart of Trinitarian Life. It is a term and a vision that sees glory as *kenosis*: a way of being proper "not only to the God who became Man, but even before that to the Creator who, by creating, penetrates into nothingness, and of the Holy Spirit also, who conceals himself 'under all kinds of rags and tatters', and 'under the rubbish' of the letter of Scripture, in such a way that truly enlightened and enthusiastic eyes are needed to 'recognize the rays of heavenly splendor dressed in such a disguise'." See Balthasar, *The Glory of the Lord: A Theological Aesthetics: Seeing the Form*, I, 80.

recall similar remarks by the crowd when He appeared in the synagogue: "many who heard him were astonished, saying, 'Where did this man get all this? What is the wisdom given to him?'" (Mk. 6:2; cf. Mt. 13:54). Amazement quickly turns to skepticism, however, for even at this tender age of twelve, the child Jesus threatens to upset the system. "Christ is the wisdom of God [and] the foolishness of God is wiser than men, and the weakness of God is stronger than men" (1 Cor. 1:24–25). This truth is already beginning to dawn on the doctors of the Law, not without a hint of scandal.

As the Word of God Incarnate, Jesus is already functioning as "a two-edge sword," separating the marrow from the bone of Israelite religion (cf. Heb. 4:12). Already he is slicing to ribbons the sacrificial nomos of Temple worship. He is unveiling the lie underlying the scapegoat ritual. He is unmasking our propensity to murder in order to establish and support the religious and social *status quo*. Incomprehensible to those who saw Him there that day, the child Jesus presents an unheard-of challenge to the Temple of Solomon. In His Wisdom He surpasses both Solomon and His Temple, for "...something greater than Solomon is here" (Mt. 12:42). Compared to the Wisdom of this Child, St. Paul considered Israelite religion as "a loss...as so much rubbish" (Phil. 3:8). The appearance of God's Child in the Temple on this day was the beginning of a full eclipse of the Tradition. His "sitting among the teachers" portends His apocalyptic appearance as the *Pantokrator* of the universe.

"And his mother said to him, 'Son, why have you done this to us? Your father and I have been looking for you with great anxiety.'"

Was there irritation in Mary's voice, in her heart, as she uttered these words? Perhaps. Was she upset? Clearly. Her words remind us of Jesus' disciples when, amidst a storm on the Sea of Galilee, the pleaded with Him, "Do you no care that we are perishing?!" (Mk. 4:38). Or of Martha in Bethany when she asked of Jesus, "Lord, do you not care that my sister has left me by myself to do the serving?" (Lk 10:40). Yet Mary's words are also shot through with the same innocent openness that characterized her question to Gabriel at the Annunciation: "How can this be since I know not man?" (Lk. 1:34). Not a trace of doubt, not a shred of unbelief, only a virginal question, an innocent request for clarification.

We are also reminded here of the tenor of her statement to Jesus at the Wedding Feast at Cana: "They have no wine" (Jn. 2:3). Here again Mary is simply laying bare the movements of her heart before Jesus. With total trust and fearless candor, she makes know to her Son the deepest feelings in her soul. No accusation, no expectation of any specific response, only the perfect confidence in His love that entrusts to Him the anxiety she is feeling.

Being a disciple - and Mary is the first of His disciples - means always having our vision adjusted to accommodate the Ever-greater revelation of Jesus. The gospel is never about us. It is always all about Him. Though well-intentioned, Mary's question to Jesus is misdirected. It is not really about *"what you have done to us."* Rather, it is about what Jesus is doing *in response to what His Father desires.* Even

Mary had to learn that Christian discipleship is continually adjusting our minds and hearts to the One who comes to us from above (Jn. 8:23; cf. 3:31; 19:11).

Faith seeking understanding (*'fides quaerens intellectum'*) means always bursting and reconfiguring our spiritual imagination to make way for the Priority of Christ.[126] It means developing an eschatological orientation, an anagogical imagination.[127] Just as Jesus was being continually pulled forward and upward by the Will of His Father, so are we, like Mary, pulled forward and upward in our understanding of Jesus by allowing our minds and hearts to be bewildered, de-constructed, and re-created by His Holy Spirit.

Mary and Joseph have been *"searching for [Jesus]* "*with great anxiety."* All anxiety, in truth, is a function of our searching for Jesus. Jesus is "the Way, the Truth, and the Life" (Jn. 14:6). He is the *Logos* of creation, the Cornerstone of History. He Key *Hypothesis* in light of which all historical events cohere.[128] He is the Centerpiece of the world. All things find their security only in Him. "He holds all things together in Himself" (Col. 1:17), reconciling in His very Person "all things in heaven and on earth" (Col. 1:20). Remove the Lord from the mix and everything collapses. All comes to naught that is not connected to Him. Anxiety is the natural condition of whose who have not discovered Jesus.

We are human thirsts. We are created as inherently incomplete creatures. Our hearts are restless, as St. Augustine said, until they rest in God. We are drawn, in the center of our hearts, to we-know-not-where. "It is not good for man to be alone" (Gen. 2:18). But even marriage is not the final answer to the intrinsic incompleteness that defines our being human. Marriage is a sacrament - a sign - of the more primordial marriage, a more mystical communion for which

---

[126] See the excellent book by Bishop Robert Barron by the same title, *The Priority of Christ*.

[127] See my book, *Deified Vision: Towards an Anagogical Catholicism*.

[128] See above, n. 96. See also Gregory A. Boyd, *Crucifixion of the Warrior God*, vol. 1, 40ff.

we are created. This mystical marriage is the Wedding Feast of the Lamb: the *apokatastasis* of the entire created order with the Triune God.

At the end of His life on earth, of course, Jesus will give us the Eucharist as an image and a foretaste of this Wedding Feast of the Lamb. But even then our anagogical hunger will receive only an anticipatory share in the satisfaction we seek. The fulness of God's glory will always remain hidden beneath the simple signs of bread and wine. Moments of transfiguration will always appear as temporary, the miracle of transubstantiation will always seem somewhat banal. The Eucharist is a *proleptic* presence of the Consummation we seek: already here but not yet complete.

Our seeking of Jesus will continue even in the world to come. True, at that time "He will wipe every tear from their eyes, and there shall be no more death or mourning, wailing or pain, for the old order has passed away" (Rev. 21:4), and we shall see Him "face to face" and "[we] shall know fully, as [we are] fully known" (1 Cor. 13:12). But, even in the Father's Kingdom, our hunger for Jesus will be no less intense. We will no longer experience the anxiety of losing Him, but we will experience an *ever-exceeding desire* and a never-ending delight in imbibing ever-more of His ever-giving Love. The manifestation of His Divine Majesty is ever-surprising and never-ending in the Kingdom of God. The Wedding Feast of the Lamb exacerbates the very appetite for the Father's Love that our communion with Jesus there perpetually satisfies.

*"He said to them, 'Why did you search for Me? Did you
not know I had to be in my Father's house?'"*

We can discern here a combination of adolescent immaturity, perhaps, and Jesus' divine preoccupation with the desires of His Father.
His supernatural sensitivity to the things of the Father render Him
relatively indifferent to the concerns of His earthly parents. Was
something of the prophet Isaiah speaking to Jesus that day?: *"My
thoughts are not your thoughts, nor are your ways my ways, says the Lord. For
as the heavens are higher than the earth, so are my ways higher than your ways,
my thoughts higher than your thoughts"* (Isa. 55:8–9). Perhaps an element
of teenage insensitivity, combined with His divine inspiration, made
Jesus unaware of how such true but severe language would have
impacted Joseph and Mary?

Jesus Himself is searching for no one, save perhaps sinners who
know neither Him nor His Father (Lk. 19:10). "Seek," He admon-
ishes us, "and you shall find" (Mt. 7:7). Jesus is a Finder, not a Seeker.
He seeks only to know and to do His Father's Will (Jn. 4:34), thus
all lesser concerns are of little or no concern to Him (cf. Jn. 2:4).

Somehow Jesus senses His Father's Presence in the Temple and
calls it "My Father's House." All the world, of course, is the Father's
house, but the *Shekinah* of God seemed to find its special resting
place in the Temple on Mt. Zion in Jerusalem. The Temple seemed
the preferred location where the Cloud of the Father's Presence now
encompassed the faithful in Israel. Did the twelve-year-old Jesus
experience in the Temple that day an anticipatory touch of the the-
ophanic Presence that would later envelop Him in the River Jordan

(Mt. 3:17) and on the summit of Mt. Tabor (Mt. 17:5)? Did Jesus experience Himself there as the Father's "Beloved Son," such as He would hear the Father later declare (Mt. 17:5)? Was His experience of the Father's Presence in the Temple so overwhelming that He was rendered temporarily insensitive to the feelings of Joseph and Mary?

Prophetically, we might imagine Jesus speaking thus to Mary and Joseph: "Why, O mother and father, do you worry? Don't you understand that in My Father's House neither fear nor death exist? My Rest is to abide in My Father's House, to abide in the invisible Embrace of His never-ending Love. I am His Beloved. In Me, you too are beloved of Him. No one can come to Me unless My Father draws him (Jn. 6:65). I will lose nothing of what My Father has given Me (Jn. 6:39). Abiding in My Father Love is everything for Me. You are alive only to the extent that you abide in Me, even as I abide in Him (cf. Jn. 17:21-26).

"All of this, dear Mary, dear Joseph, is hidden from your view as I sit here amidst the doctors of Law. The curtain in the Temple is not yet torn (Mk. 15:38). The parapets of the Temple are not yet destroyed (Mt. 24:2). In those days you will know that I am He who existed before Abraham was (Jn. 8:58). Then I will wipe away every tear (Rev. 17:7; 214) and you will see me clearly, no longer as through a mirror dimly (1 Cor. 13:12). Until such time you will search for me with great anxiety. But be of good cheer, dear mother and father, for I have overcome the world!" (Jn. 16:33).

"But they did not grasp what He said to them..."

God's Wisdom is darkness to us. Yet, this "darkness" is an effulgence, an excess of Light. As St. John of the Cross says: Divine Wisdom is experienced as darkness "because the height of Divine Wisdom exceeds the abilities of the soul; and on this account the wisdom is dark for the soul...[for] the clearer and more obvious divine things are in themselves, the darker and more hidden they are to the soul naturally. The brighter the light, the more the owl is blinded; and the more one looks at the brilliant sun, the more the sun darkens the faculty of sight, deprives and overwhelms it in its weakness."[129]

John of the Cross goes on to note that "because the light and wisdom [of God] is very bright and pure...the soul in which it sines...will be deeply afflicted on receiving it...and suffer immensely at the time this divine light truly assails it."[130] This could account, in part, for the anxious, painful bewilderment suffered by Joseph and Mary at the incomprehensible actions of their twelve-year old Son. Jesus is a Mystery, a Divine Enigma, even to those who are closest to Him. "No one knows the Son except the Father, and no one knows the Father except the Son and anyone to whom the Son wishes to reveal him" (Mt. 11:27).

Everything Jesus says and does is quite beyond human comprehension. As Joseph and Mary discovered that day in the Temple, not only are "My ways not your ways," but "as the heavens are higher

---

[129] *Dark Night of the Soul*, II, V, 3-5.
[130] Ibid.

than the earth, so are …my thoughts higher than your thoughts" (Isa. 55:9). Divine Wisdom forever transcends the human intellect. God cannot be understood or comprehended. He can only be encountered, listened to, believed in, loved, obeyed, and enjoyed. Anything else is but human make-believe.

Even though His Light is darkness to us, it is only *in light of His Light* that we see light (Ps. 36:9-10). The incomprehensible *Logos* of God - Jesus, the Eternal Word - is the unfathomable Light illumining all created things. Science is made possible by the Mystery of the Eternal Word (*Logos*). Because He reveals God as *Logos*, Jesus affirms to the world that there is coherence, predictability, and rationality in the structures of the created order. As Pope Benedict XVI has said, "what happens here [in this world] is not a blind surrender to the irrational. On the contrary, it is a movement toward the *logos*, the *ratio*, toward meaning and so toward truth itself, for in the final analysis the ground on which man takes his stand cannot possibly be anything else but the truth revealing itself."[131] Hence St. Paul could say: "For in him were created all things in heaven and on earth, the visible and the invisible, whether thrones or dominions or principalities or powers; all things were created through him and for him." (Col. 1:16).

To "find Jesus" is to discover that we never really know Him. It is to find out that there is always infinitely more to discover about Him. Like Mary and Joseph that day in the Temple, to find Jesus is always to come upon an Divine Mystery that far exceeds our finite comprehension. "Who is this," we ask, who confounds and intrigues the doctors of the Law? "Who is this" who chides his parents for not naturally discerning His mission? "Who do you say that I am?," he will later ask His disciples (Mk. 8:27).

We seek Jesus as we might seek the horizon: the closer we seem to get, the further away the it appears. Yet the breadth and depth

---

[131] Joseph Ratzinger, *Introduction to Christianity*, 75.

of the far horizon continue to beckon us forward. Its beauty and grandeur draw us closer ever more completely.

We seek Jesus because He is already seeking us (cf. Ps. 139:4; Jn. 15:16). We seek Him because He has first sought for us (cf. 1 Jn. 4:19). Man's quest for God is the unwitting response to God's search for man.[132] God became man in Jesus so men and women could become God in Him.[133] This marvelous exchange (*admirable commercium*) is still very little known among the People of God, especially among those who believe they have found Jesus in their religion. For neither religion nor ritual, neither creed nor cult, neither temple nor church can contain the Eternal Word incarnate in the 12-year old Jesus.

The Mysteries of Joy reveal the sort of joy the Mystery of Jesus imparts. They constitute a revelation and a joy that cause us to catch our breath. The Word Incarnate contradicts all our views of what makes logical, human sense. Jesus appears in our world at His Father's *Logos,* His Divine Logic, a power and wisdom that overshadows and exceeds, condemns and redeems all of our normal ways of approaching life. The Divine Wisdom bewilders us before it delights us, it baffles us before it makes things clear to us.

The Joy that Jesus brings can only be had by humble hearts. For it has not pleased the Father to reveal His Son to "the wise and learned," but only to "the childlike" (Lk. 10:21), i.e., to those who, like the shepherds, His Mother, and the Magi, approach Him in humble adoration. He has "chosen the foolish of the world to shame the wise, and the weak to shame the strong" (1 Cor. 1:27).

---

[132] See the marvelous works of Abraham Heschel: *Man's Quest for God* and *God in Search of Man.*

[133] See above, n. 57.

*"He went down with them then, and came to
Nazareth, and was obedient to them."*

As quickly as His glory flashes forth in the Temple, just as swiftly
does it disappear behind the docility of the twelve-year old boy.
Another twenty years or so of silence now envelops Him. Jesus
goes into hiding, as it were, yet He is maturing into the mission His
appearance in the Temple prefigures.

What were they thinking as they returned to Nazareth? Was
Mary recalling her first trip to Ein Kerem - that blessed encounter
with her cousin Elizabeth - when the baby leapt in Elizabeth's womb
for joy and Mary sang her Magnificat prayer of praise? Or was she
already imagining another trip to Judea, this time to fulfill her own
mission as one whose heart will be pierced by a sword?

And what about Joseph the Silent?[134] He and Jesus seem to be of
a piece in their disposition at this point: Jesus enfolded in His foster-father's quietude, the deep, still waters of Joseph's contemplative
spirit blending together with the Living Water inundating the heart,
mind, and soul of his Son.

And what did Nazareth look like when the Holy Family returned? How did their hometown appear to them following the
mini-theophany they had witnessed in Jerusalem? When one has
been to the mountain top, level ground never looks the same again.
Things are relativized in light of an elevated vision. Atop Mt. Zion,
Jesus had just given Joseph and Mary the smallest taste of the glory
contained in His Divine Person. Later, atop Mt. Tabor, He would

---

[134] See the beautiful book by Michel Gasnier O.P., *Joseph the Silent.*

manifest a fuller share of His divine nature to Peter, James, and John. In both experiences, the participants are transfigured. They can never forget what "we have seen and heard" (cf. Acts 4:20). They are now His witnesses, witnesses of "his dwelling among us. We have seen his glory, the glory as of the Father's only Son, full of grace and truth" (Jn. 1:14).

No mountain is required for us to behold the glory of the Only-begotten Son. His every word, His simplest action is a revelation of God's divine glory. Even His silence, suffering, and death are manifestations of that fathomless *pistis Christou* - faithfulness to His Father - that constitute the *glory* of His Sonship. "Behold, I make all things new," says the Redeemer (Rev. 21:5). No where is this assertion more paradoxically verified than in the humble hiddenness Jesus' glory now assumes as *"He goes down with them, and comes to Nazareth."*

Consummate humility is the hallmark of the Lord. Hiddenness is at the heart of His revelation. Even in the fulness of His Incarnation, He remains shrouded in Mystery. To know Him intimately is to realize that we know Him very little indeed. His beauty ever-exceeds our encounter with His Presence.

Obedience means 'listening' (from Latin: *ob*-towards + *oedire* (akin to *audire* to hear). It connotes openness, receptivity. Jesus is open, receptive to the life of the Father. The Father Himself is Total Surrender, complete Self-Emptying. Everything the Father has and is He pours forth into His Eternal Word (Jn. 17:10). For His part, the Son is all receptivity. Everything He has and is Jesus acknowledges as a gift from His Father (Jn. 17:10; cf. 8:38). He, in turn, becomes complete Self-Emptying (*kenosis*). Just as the fulness of His Father's Life is poured out into His Son, so too does Jesus pour out all of His life into us.

"We become God," writes St. Maximus the Confessor, "in the same measure as God became man."[135] We become "partakers of

---

[135] Cited in D. B. Clendenin, *Eastern Orthodox Christianity: A Western Perspective*, 131.

His divine nature" (2 Pt. 1:4), gods by participation with Jesus in His communion with His Father. We also become partakers in His consummate humility. His *kenosis* is our *theosis*...which, in turn, makes us participants in His own kenotic self-emptying. We enter joyfully into Christ's poverty of spirit. We enter joyfully into His receptivity to His Father. We enter joyfully into His filial devotion to Mary, His Mother.

> *"His mother kept all these things in her heart. And Jesus advanced in wisdom and age and favor before God and man."*

Mary allows the ineffable Light of Jesus' actions penetrate and enter her heart. She is illumined from within by a contemplation inspired by the Holy Spirit. She is a House of Gold: the widows of her soul radiant with Light from beyond. The 'Beyond of God' is within the heart of Mary. He is in her and she is in Him. Mary is the prototype of the Church and of every Christian. She is the model of the mutual indwelling that her Son desired: *"that they may all be one, as you, Father, are in me and I in you, that they also may be in us, that the world may believe that you sent me"* (Jn. 17:21).

To contemplate the dramatic details of Jesus' life is to make contact with that Life itself. It is the Holy Spirit who inspires both our meditation and contemplation. The *anamnesis* (remembrance) of Jesus is also always an instantiation of Him in the present moment. *"Where two or three are gathered in My Name, behold, there I am in their midst"* (Mt. 18:20). The Holy Spirit 'calls Jesus to mind' only to 'make Him present' to those who call upon Him and contemplate Him.[136] Contemplation is always a participation in the very Personhood of Jesus. Contemplation is our means of incorporation into His Communion with His Father. All of Christianity is a participation in the Person and Prayer of Jesus.[137] Thus, Mary is the foremost

---

[136] On the mystery of *anamnesis* and the fourfold action of the Holy Spirit in relation to it, see CCC 1103-1109.

[137] The Divine Personhood of Jesus *is* the Prayer of Jesus, i.e., it defines the relationality of the Son to the Father. As Pope Benedict XVI says, "Since the center of the person of Jesus is prayer, it is essential to participate in his prayer if we are to know

Christian and the first Christian contemplative. She is more intimately united to Him as she contemplates Him in her heart than she is when holding Him in her arms.

By *"advancing in wisdom and age before God and man,"* Jesus gathers up and recapitulates (i.e., summarizes, perfects and redeems) every dimension and aspect of being human. He deifies human growth stages, making them portals, as it were, for the human person such that at every moment and transition in life we can enter into communion with God, not by fleeing or evading the twists and turns of being human, but by embracing them as our God-given opportunities for acceptance and conversion. "All things work for good," St. Paul tells us, "for those who love God" (Rom. 8:28). The "passing through" of Jesus of all the stages and dimensions of human maturation makes of those stages and dimensions divinely blessed loci for the spiritual growth and development of the human person. The Eternal Word sanctifies every aspect of being human as he *"advances in wisdom and age before God and man."*

Ultimately it is the experience of death that is most paradoxically divinized by the Passage of Jesus through its forbidding doors. He does so by *embracing* death, not by 'suffering' it or simply 'undergoing' it like a helpless victim. "Earnestly have I desired to eat this

and understand him….the central act of the person of Jesus and, indeed, that this person is constituted by the act of prayer, of unbroken communication with the one he calls "Father". If this is the case, it is only possible really to understand this person by entering into this act of prayer, by participating in it. This is suggested by Jesus' saying that no one can come to him unless the Father draws him (Jn 6:44). Where there is no Father, there is no Son. Where there is no relationship with God, there can be no understanding of him who, in his innermost self, is nothing but relationship with God, the Father—although one can doubtless establish plenty of details about him. Therefore a participation in the mind of Jesus, i.e., in his prayer, which (as we have seen) is an act of love, of self-giving and self-expropriation to men, is not some kind of pious supplement to reading the Gospels, adding nothing to knowledge of him or even being an obstacle to the rigorous purity of critical knowing. On the contrary, it is the basic precondition if real understanding, in the sense of modern hermeneutics—i.e., the entering-in to the same time and the same meaning—is to take place." *Behold the Pierced One: An Approach to a Spiritual Christology*, 25-26.

Passover with you before I suffer," Jesus says (Lk. 22:11). Here He is re-affirming His earlier assertion that "[t]here is a baptism with which I must be baptized, and how great is my anguish until it is accomplished!" (Lk. 12:50). Despite the physical suffering involved, Jesus eagerly looks forward to His "Hour" (cf. Jn. 2:4; 7:30; 12:23, 27; 13:1; 17:1) when He will "disarm the powers and principalities" (Col. 2:15). They have conspired to make death a determinative principle of dread for the human race. Jesus, however, by embracing His Cross and accepting the ignominy of a horrendous death, comes to deliver from "the slavery of the fear of death" (Heb. 2:15) those who place their trust in Him. "No one takes my life from me," says the Lord, "but I lay it down of my own accord" (Jn. 10:18). The intentionality with which Jesus approaches and undergoes His own death gives the lie to death as the final word about life. Instead, the manner in which Jesus undergoes His own death reveals death, not as an ending, but as a final opportunity for all those faithful to God to exclaim with the Redeemer, "Father, into Your hands I commend my spirit!" (Lk. 23:46).

CONCLUSION

There is no limit to the joy we experience by contemplating the scenes from the life of Jesus! Every word, every action, every gesture, even His repose in death is a beautiful image and icon of the deifying love He brings to the world. The Mysteries of Joy are the *Ur-Mysteries* of the Rosary. They are fontal meditations on the early events in the life of Jesus that enable us to see the Sorrowful, Luminous, and Glorious Mysteries in light of the Joy of His Gospel. What begins with the announcement of the angelic choirs, "I proclaim to you good news of great joy that will be for all the people. For today in the city of David a savior has been born for you who is Messiah and Lord" (Lk. 2:10–11), culminates in Jesus proclaiming "Be of good cheer, I have overcome the world!" (Jn. 16:33). All is Joy when contemplating Christ, even in His ignominy on the Cross. "O death, where is thy sting, where is your victory?" (1 Cor. 15:55). The joy of St. Paul is the Joy of the Gospel, a joy that can never be undone.

SELECT BIBLIOGRAPHY

Barron, Robert. (2016). *The Priority of Christ: Towards a Postliberal Catholicism.* Grand Rapids, MI: Baker Academic.

Behr, John. (2006). *The Mystery of Christ: Life in Death.* Crestwood, NY: St. Vladimir's Seminary Press.

Benedict XVI. (2011). *Dogma and Preaching: Applying Christian Doctrine to Daily Life.* (M. J. Miller, Ed., M. J. Miller & M. J. O'Connell, Trans.) (Unabridged Edition). San Francisco: Ignatius Press.

_____. (2010). *Verbum Domini.* Vatican City: Libreria Editrice Vaticana.

_____. (2007). *Spe Salvi.* Vatican City: Libreria Editrice Vaticana.

Boersma, Hans. (2015). *Embodiment and Virtue in Gregory of Nyssa: An Anagogical Approach.* (Oxford Early Christian Studies). Oxford: Oxford University Press.

Boyd, Gregory A. (2017). The Crucifixion of the Warrior God: Volumes 1 & 2. (Combined edition). Philadelphia, PA: Fortress Press.

Bulgakov, Sergius. (2008). *The Lamb of God.* (Boris Jakim, Trans.). Grand Rapids, MI: Wm. B. Eerdmanns Publishing Co.

Clendenin, D. B. (1994). Eastern Orthodox Christianity: A Western Perspective. Grand Rapids, MI: Baker Academic.

Christensen, Michael J. and Wittung, Jeffery A., Eds. (2008). *Partakers of the Divine Nature: The History and Development of Deification in the Christian Traditions.* Grand Rapids, MI: Baker Academic Press.

Gambero, Luigi. (2005). *Mary in the Middle Ages: The Blessed Virgin Mary in the Thought of Medieval Latin Theologians.* (Thomas Buffer, Trans.). San Francisco: Ignatius Press.

Gorman, Michael J. (2009). *Inhabiting the Cruciform God: Kenosis, Justification, and Theosis In Paul's Narrative Soteriology.* Grand Rapids, MI: Wm. B. Eerdmanns Publishing Co.

Gschwandtner, Christian M. (2014). *Degrees of Givenness: On Saturation in Jean-Luc Marion.* (Indiana Series in the Philosophy of Religion). Bloomington, IN: Indiana University Press.

Guroian, Vigen. (2010). *The Melody of Faith: Theology in an Orthodox Key.* Grand Rapids, MI: Wm. B. Eerdmanns Publishing Co.).

Hahn, Scott. W. (2009). *Covenant and Communion: The Biblical Theology of Pope Benedict XVI.* Grand Rapids, MI: Brazos Press.

John of the Cross, St. (1991). *The Collected Works of St. John of the Cross.* (Kieran Kavanaugh, O.C.D. and Otilio Rodriguez, O.C.D., Trans.) Washington, D.C.: ICS Publications.

John Paul II. (2006). *Man and Woman He Created Them: A Theology of the Body.* (M. Waldstein, Trans.). Boston, MA: Pauline Books & Media.

Krill, Philip. (2017). *Life in the Trinity: A Catholic Vision of Communion and Deification.* Raleigh, NC: Lulu Publishing, Inc.

Krill, Philip. (2017). *Deified Vision: Towards an Anagogical Catholicism.* Raleigh, NC: Lulu Publishing, Inc.

Leiva-Merikakis, Erasmo. (1996–2012). *Fire of Mercy, Heart of the Word: Meditations on the Gospel according to Saint Matthew, Chapters 1–25* (Vol. 1–3). San Francisco: Ignatius Press.

Lossky, Vladimir. (2001). *In the Image and Likeness of God.* (John H. Erickson, Trans.). Crestwood, NJ: St. Vladimir's Seminary Press.

Manoussakis, John Panteleimon. (2007). *God After Metaphysics: A Theological Aesthetic.* (Indiana Series in the Philosophy of Religion). Bloomington, IN: Indiana University Press.

Marion, Jean-Luc. (1995). *God Without Being: Hors-Texte.* (Religion and Postmodernism Series). (Thomas A. Carlson, Trans.). Chicago: University of Chicago Press.

Marion, Jean-Luc. (2004). *In Excess: Studies of Saturated Phenomena.* (Perspectives in Continental Philosophy). (Robyn Horner and Vincent Berraud, Trans.).

McKenzie, S.J., John L. (1995). *Dictionary of the Bible.* (Reprint edition). New York:

Simon & Schuster (A Touchstone Book).

Merton, Thomas. (1951). *Seeds of Contemplation.* New York: Dell Publishing Co.

Merton, Thomas. (1961). *New Seeds of Contemplation.* New York: New Directions Books.

Merton, Thomas. (1999). *The New Man. (Reissue edition).* New York: Farrar, Straus and Giroux.

Minns, Denis. (2010). *Irenaeus: An Introduction.* (Revised Edition). London: T&T Clark.

Newman, John Henry. (2015). *An Essay on the Development of Christian Doctrine.* London: Aeterna Press.

O'Keefe, John J. and Reno, R. R. (2005). *Sanctified Vision: An Introduction to Early Christian Interpretation of the Bible.* Baltimore, MD: Johns Hopkins University Press.

Ratzinger, Joseph. (1986). *Behold the Pierced One: An Approach to a Spiritual Christology.* (G. Harrison, Trans.). San Francisco: Ignatius Press.

_____. (1992). *Co-Workers of the Truth: Meditations for Every Day of the Year.* (I. Grassl, Ed., M. F. McCarthy & L. Krauth, Trans.). San Francisco: Ignatius Press.

_____. (1983). *Daughter Zion: Meditations on the Church's Marian Belief.* (J. M. McDermot, Trans.). San Francisco: Ignatius Press.

_____. (2004). *Introduction to Christianity.* (J. R. Foster. Trans.) (Revised Edition). San Francisco: Ignatius Press, 2004.

_____. (2005). *On the Way to Jesus Christ.* (M. J. Miller, Trans.). San Francisco: Ignatius Press.

_____. (1987). *Principles of Catholic Theology: Building Stones for a Fundamental Theology.* (M. F. McCarthy, Trans.). San Francisco: Ignatius Press.

_____. (1993). *The Meaning of Christian Brotherhood.* San Francisco: Ignatius Press.

Ratzinger, Joseph Cardinal and Von Balthasar, Hans Urs (1997), *Mary: The Church at the Source*, (Adrian Walker, Trans.). San Francisco: Ignatius Press.

Russell, Norman. (2006). *The Doctrine of Deification in the Greek Patristic Tradition*. (Oxford Early Christian Studies). Oxford: Oxford University Press.

Schindler, D. L. (Ed.). (2008). *Love Alone Is Credible: Hans Urs von Balthasar as Interpreter of the Catholic Tradition*. Grand Rapids, MI; Cambridge, U.K.: William B. Eerdmans Publishing Company.

Schönborn, Christoph. (1994). *God's Human Face: The Christ-Icon*. (Krouth, Lothar, Trans.). San Francisco: Ignatius Press.

Von Speyr, Adrienne. (2012). *Mary in the Redemption*. (Helena M. Tomko, Trans.). San Francisco: Ignatius Press.

Speyr, Adrienne. (1987). *The World of Prayer*. (Graham Harrison, Trans.). San Francisco: Ignatius Press.

Steenberg, Matthew C. (2009). *Of God and Man: Theology as Anthropology from Irenaeus to Athanasius*. Edinburgh: Bloomsbury T&T Clark, 1st edition.

Stendahl, Krister. (1963). *"The Apostle Paul and the Introspective Conscience of the West."* Harvard Theological Review 56, 199-215.

Tallon, Andrew. (1997). *Head and Heart: Affection, Cognition, Volition as Triune Consciousness*. New York: Fordham University Press.

Von Balthasar, Hans Urs. (1993). *Explorations in Theology: Creator Spirit*. (B. McNeil, Trans.) (Vol. III). San Francisco: Ignatius Press.

_____. (1995). *The Grain of Wheat: Aphorisms.* (Erasmo Leiva-Merikakas, Trans.). San Francisco: Ignatius Press.

_____. (1991). *The Glory of the Lord, a Theological Aesthetics: The Realm of Metaphysics in the Modern Age.* (O. Davies, A. Louth, B. McNeil, J. Saward, & R. Williams, Trans.) (Vol. 5). San Francisco; New York: Ignatius Press; Crossroads Publications.

_____. (1998). *Theo-Drama: Theological Dramatic Theory: The Last Act.* (G. Harrison, Trans.) (Vol. 5). San Francisco: Ignatius Press.

_____. (2000). *Theo-Logic: Theological Logical Theory: The Truth of the World.* (A. J. Walker, Trans.) (Vol. 1). San Francisco: Ignatius Press.

_____. (2004). *Theo-Logic: Theological Logical Theory: Truth of God.* (A. J. Walker, Trans.) (Vol. 2). San Francisco: Ignatius Press.

_____. (2005). *Theo-Logic: Theological Logical Theory: The Spirit of the Truth.* (G. Harrison, Trans.) (Vol. 3). San Francisco: Ignatius Press.

Wright, N. T. (2013). *Pauline Perspectives: Essays on Paul, 1978–2013.* Minneapolis, MN: Fortress Press.

Writings from the Philokalia on the Prayer of the Heart. (1951). (E. Kadloubovsky and G.E.H. Palmer, Trans.). London: Faber and Faber.